The 30,000-Pound Gorilla In The Room

The 30,000-Pound Gorilla In The Room

The 212 Most Annoying Business Phrases Managers Effuse, Confuse, and Overuse

A reference manual to maintain your sanity in the workplace

STEVE STAUNING
CARSON STAUNING

© 2020 by Steve Stauning & Carson Stauning
Written by: Steve Stauning & Carson Stauning
Cartoons by: Steve Stauning & Carson Stauning
Interior Illustrations by: Collette Vergon; © 2020 Steve Stauning & Carson Stauning
Cover Illustration by: D.T. Walsh; © 2020 Steve Stauning & Carson Stauning

All rights reserved under the Pan-American and International Copyright Conventions.

Printed in the USA

This book may not be reproduced in whole or in part, in any form or by any means, electronic or mechanical, including photocopying, recording, or by any information storage and/or retrieval system now known or hereafter invented, without prior written permission from the author, who holds all copyright to the written words and illustrations.

Although the authors and publisher have made every effort to ensure that the information in this book was correct at press time, the authors and publisher do not assume and hereby disclaim any liability to any party for any loss, damage, or disruption caused by errors or omissions, whether such errors or omissions result from negligence, accident, or any other cause.

In some instances, the authors tried to recreate events, locales, and conversations from their memories of them. In order to maintain anonymity in all instances, the authors changed the names and perhaps even the sex of individuals, and also altered the timelines and places the events took place (without altering the intention or meaning). Additionally, the authors may have changed some identifying characteristics and details such as physical properties, occupations, and industries.

ISBN: 9798633752588

Independently Published

Also by Steve Stauning: *Sh*t Sandwich* & *Assumptive Selling*

We wrote this book for the millions of employees in the world forced to work with the hordes of annoying managers whose tired office jargon and other clichés flow like a river from their collective pie holes.

Of course, without these irritating souls we'd have nothing to write about. So, while many friends and family helped with this book, we're reserving all our thanks for those managers who make our ears bleed.

- Steve Stauning & Carson Stauning

CONTENTS #-F

24/7 and 24/7/365 • 6
30,000-Foot View • 8
800-Pound Gorilla • 10
80/20 Rule • 12
Action Item • 14
Agree to Disagree • 16
All Hands on Deck • 18
Analysis Paralysis • 20
Are Two Different Things • 22
ASAP • 24
Ask, The • 26
At the End of the Day • 28
At This Juncture/At This Point in Time • 30
Baby is Ugly • 32
Back to Square One • 34
Back to the Drawing Board • 36
Ballpark • 38
Bandwidth • 40
Bean Counter • 42
Beat a Dead Horse • 44
Been There, Done That • 46
Behind the Eight Ball • 48
Best Thing Since Sliced Bread • 50
Between a Rock and a Hard Place • 52
Bio Break • 54
Blocking and Tackling • 56
Boots on the Ground • 58
Bottleneck • 60
Bottom Line • 62
Bring Your 'A' Game • 64
Bubble it Up • 66
Bullet-Point Me Something • 68
Burn the Boats • 70
Buy-In • 72
Cascade • 74
Change Agent • 76

Chasing Shiny Objects • 78
Circle Back • 80
Circular Firing Squad • 82
Client Engagement • 84
Come to Jesus Meeting • 86
Coming Down the Pike (Pipe?) • 88
Connect With • 90
Could Care Less • 92
Crawl, Walk, Run • 94
Cross the T's and Dot the I's • 96
Crushing It • 98
Currently Now • 100
Cut the Mustard • 102
Dead in the Water • 104
Deliverables • 106
Devil is in the Detail • 108
Direct the Traffic • 110
Disruptor • 112
Do a Deep Dive • 114
Dog in this Fight • 116
Double-Edged Sword • 118
Download • 120
Drill Down • 122
Drink from a Firehose • 124
Drink/Drank the Kool-Aid • 126
Drop-Dead Date • 128
Drop the Ball • 130
Ducks in a Row • 132
Easier Said than Done • 134
Eat Your Own Dog Food • 136
Elephant in the Room • 138
Face Time • 140
Firewalled • 142
Full-Court Press • 144
FYI • 146

CONTENTS G-P

Game Changer • 148
Game Plan • 150
Game Time • 152
Get into Bed • 154
Give 110% • 156
Give You a Heads Up • 158
Go Forward Basis • 160
Go-Getter • 162
Go Slow to Go Fast • 164
Goes Without Saying • 166
Good with a Hammer • 168
Grind • 170
Guru • 172
Hack • 174
Hail Mary • 176
Hammer it Out • 178
Hard Stop • 180
Haters Gonna Hate • 182
Headhunter • 184
Heavy Lifting • 186
Herding Cats • 188
Hit the Ground Running • 190
Hit the Nail on the Head • 192
Holding Hands • 194
How the Sausage is Made • 196
Hustle • 198
If It Ain't Broke Don't Fix It • 200
Impact • 202
Incremental Improvement • 204
It Is What It Is • 206
It's a Cart and Horse Situation • 208
It's All in the Details • 210
It's all Semantics • 212
It's not Rocket Science/It's not Brain Surgery • 214
Jack of All Trades, Master of None • 216
Juice is not/is Worth the Squeeze • 218

Jumped the Shark • 220
Keep me Looped-In • 222
Land the Plane • 224
Let Me Start by Saying • 226
Level Set • 228
Light a Fire Under • 230
Line in the Sand • 232
Literally • 234
Lost in the Sauce • 236
Low-Hanging Fruit • 238
Make the Cut • 240
Minefields • 242
Mission Critical • 244
Move the Goalposts • 246
Move the Needle • 248
My Two Cents • 250
Net-Net • 252
Next Level • 254
No Problem • 256
Not my First Rodeo • 258
Nothing Burger • 260
Of the World, The (Blanks) • 262
On Our Radar • 264
On the Same Page • 266
One-Trick Pony • 268
Open a Dialogue • 270
Operationalize • 272
Optics • 274
Out-of-Pocket • 276
Over the Line • 278
Ownership • 280
Par for the Course • 282
Paradigm Shift • 284
Pass Muster • 286
Pass the Buck • 288

CONTENTS P-Z (sort of)

Pee in your Pool • 290
Piece, The (Blank) • 292
Pick Up the Ball and Run with It • 294
Ping • 296
Play Ball • 298
Play Hardball • 300
Playing Phone Tag • 302
Point Person • 304
Postmortem • 306
Price Point • 308
Pull Yourself Up By Your Bootstraps • 310
Push the Envelope • 312
Put a Pin in It • 314
Put it on the Back Burner • 316
Putting Out Fires • 318
Raise the Bar • 320
Reaching Out • 322
Reinvent the Wheel • 324
Riding Shotgun • 326
Rightsizing • 328
Rising Tide Lifts all Boats • 330
Run Interference • 332
Run it up the Flagpole • 334
Screw the Pooch • 336
Seamless Integration • 338
Shit Hits the Fan • 340
Shit the Bed • 342
Shit Where You Eat • 344
Show the Seams • 346
Silos • 348
Skin in the Game • 350
Smell Test • 352
So • 354
Solutions Provider • 356
Soup to Nuts • 358

Space • 360
Spinning the Plates • 362
Stake in the Ground • 364
Stay in Your Lane • 366
Sync • 368
Synergistically • 370
Take it Offline • 372
Take it Up/Down a Notch • 374
Team Player • 376
Tear Down, The • 378
Tee it Up • 380
That Said • 382
There's a First Time for Everything • 384
There is No "I" in Team • 386
Think Outside the Box • 388
Thought Leader • 390
Total-Total • 392
Touch Base • 394
Transition Phase • 396
Triage • 398
Troops • 400
Trying to Boil the Ocean • 402
Under the Bus • 404
Unpack • 406
Up to Speed • 408
Utilize/Utilization • 410
Warts and All • 412
Waterfall • 414
What Keeps You Up at Night • 416
Wheelhouse • 418
Where the Rubber Meets the Road • 420
Win-Win Scenario • 422
Work Smarter, Not Harder • 424
Wrap Your Head Around • 426
You Don't Know What You Don't Know • 428

"Sometimes I'll start a sentence, and I don't even know where it's going. I just hope I find it along the way."

Michael Scott, *The Office* (2008)

THE 30,000-POUND GORILLA IN THE ROOM

STEVE STAUNING
CARSON STAUNING

Motivation for *The 30,000-Pound Gorilla*

In 2008, after decades of listening to knucklehead managers spout the most annoying analogies, clichés, and other jargon, I posted an article titled "The 25 Most Annoying Business Phrases" on my *AskTheManager.com* business and leadership blog. The post was more of an attempt at catharsis than anything else. It felt good to write it.

The post languished for years; occasionally enjoying large, though short-lived spikes in traffic whenever shared. That is, until 2015, when the average monthly visits to the page grew above 2,000.

Two thousand visitors in a month to a blog post isn't all that significant for many bloggers; however, the traffic never again waned – it grew.

Watching the demand increase for this old post, I realized there were millions of others in the workplace growing tired of listening to this endless stream of irritating sayings. So, I enlisted my oldest son Carson to help me build the ultimate guide to annoying business jargon – hoping, of course, to deliver the same cathartic effect to others.

While compiling our list of phrases, the biggest question for us became what to call this thing.

Fortunately, I remembered a cringe-worthy moment from an important meeting held more than ten years prior. In this meeting, an up-and-coming young manager where I was working told a group of peers and senior executives, "I think it's time we all addressed the 30,000-pound gorilla in the room."

The room fell silent… the awkwardness grew… the young manager shut his mouth for the rest of the meeting… and the perfect title for this book was born!

From the meaningless to the overused to the clichéd, we are inundated daily with annoying and ridiculous business phrases from the lips of otherwise well-meaning (and not-so-well-meaning) professionals.

Why so many of us (present company included) rely on the latest catch phrases or tired business jargon to relay a simple message is unclear. Whether lazy, blocked, or we just think it makes us sound important, we too often reach for prepackaged word groupings instead of constructing an original thought.

Perhaps this book can help us quit… though I doubt it.

- Steve

30,000-Pound Gorilla

"If they're committed 24/7, I'll make sure Gunnar is there 25/8, dammit!"

24/7 and 24/7/365

When describing the operating hours of your local 7-11 or Denny's restaurant, *24/7* or even *24/7/365* is appropriate. However, when a manager overuses either of these to describe his or her alleged commitment to a project – or worse, the unrealistic dedication they expect from their team – their message loses all meaning.

"We're going to be on this *24/7/365*," they assure the client. Meanwhile, their team rolls their eyes and prepares to carry the impossible load their manager just committed them to. What's most interesting about those managers who make these *24/7* commitments is they generally are the last to arrive in the morning and first to leave.

Of course, they see themselves as dedicated, thoughtful, and hardworking leaders; while their subordinates know the opposite is true. As everyone who's ever worked for one of these lazy task masters knows: talk is cheap, and actions speak volumes.

About the only enjoyment we envision you can receive from hearing some manager spout, "We're going to be on this *24/7*," is to quickly add, "Like white on rice!" to the end of his or her sentence. This usually raises an approving nod from your clueless manager and a knowing smile from your coworkers. #Victory

Replacement phrases: No replacement phrase needed. Like most overused manager sayings, this one is mostly unnecessary. If you're looking for a way to say you're committed to something or a project is in good hands, just say, "We're committed" or, "It's in good hands."

See also: *Give 110%*

30,000-Pound Gorilla

"I'm not sure getting the actual 30,000-foot view was really all that important!"

30,000-Foot View

This annoying phrase often has its annoyance factor magnified by those who don't understand its meaning or origin. A *30,000-foot view* is simply meant to describe the view from a commercial airplane (flying, of course, at 30,000 feet).

However, when used in business, its intention is to convey the notion that someone is considering everything; that is, they see the big picture.

The phrase is most often uttered by pompous managers who believe they see and consider the whole shebang, while the rest of us are too small-minded or too focused on the minutia to understand much beyond our current five-foot-eleven-inch view.

Of course, because so many don't fully understand where the saying originated, you'll often hear businesspeople refer to a 5,000-foot view, a 100,000-foot view, and everything in between.

While writing this book, we even heard a television journalist discussing, "The 65,000-foot view."

Clearly, he enjoys more than twice the vision of the average reporter… or your pompous manager.

Replacement phrases: The Big Picture. (We know this is also clichéd, but at least everyone will understand the meaning.)

See also: *Land the Plane*

Koko lost 300 pounds on Nutri-Simian!

800-Pound Gorilla

Just as the distance can vary with the *30,000-Foot View*, so too can the weight (and species) of our gorilla. Over the course of Steve's business career, he's been warned of the 300-pound gorilla and the 5,000-pound gorilla and the 30,000-pound gorilla. Strangely, he's also been told not to upset the 2,000-pound elephant in the room.

What?

However, the most interesting multivariable misuse of this phrase happened over a decade ago when an up-and-coming young manager told a group of his peers and some senior executives in a large meeting, "I think it's time we all addressed the 30,000-pound gorilla in the room."

This came out of nowhere, and the young manager didn't bother to explain why or even to whom he was referring when he described this King Kong-like, fifteen-ton behemoth. He just said it; then appeared to regret he said it; then (thankfully) shut his mouth for the rest of the meeting.

(Of course, we're thrilled Steve was present when that young manager uttered this creative mash-up; otherwise we would've struggled for an appropriate title for this book.)

This saying, of course, is meant to describe someone or something so powerful they seem unbeatable. We've heard this phrase used to describe tough competitors, tough customers, and tough bosses. Given its various meanings, it usually cannot be uttered without also mentioning the associated gorilla (competitor, customer, boss), making its annoying overuse also annoyingly redundant.

Replacement phrases: Tough competitor; Market leader

See also: *Elephant in the Room*

30,000-Pound Gorilla

"Eaton takes the 80/20 Rule to heart. He lets out 80% of his frustration on 20% of his employees."

80/20 Rule

The *80/20 Rule* is an informal restating of something called the Pareto Principle, which means (in many instances) about 80% of the outcomes are derived from roughly 20% of the sources. An example of this rule, when used correctly, might be when a company enjoys 80% of its revenue from just 20% of the products it offers.

Other correct uses apply to affluence (roughly 80% of the wealth in the world is likely controlled by about 20% of the population) and to health care (where 80% of the medical resources might be used by just 20% of the patients).

Of course, if always used correctly, the *80/20 Rule* would never deserve a page in this book. Thank goodness we have managers out there applying the *80/20 Rule* to anything and everything – and often just thrown out there as an answer by itself.

"Oh, well, you know… that's the old *80/20 Rule*, right?"

The key to remember when we're talking about statistical information (like anything one might assume fits the *80/20 Rule*) is that 92% of people believe 76% of statistics are made up on the spot. Of course, anyone who truly understands the *80/20 Rule* knows 80% of the fake statistics are made up by just 20% of the people.

Replacement phrases: There is no replacement phrase; as the *80/20 Rule* is fine when used correctly. Unfortunately, it seems 80% of the correct uses come from just 20% of the people who utter it.

See also: *Incremental Improvement*

"Wow, Marvel's really trying to squeeze all they can out of the Avengers' franchise."

Action Item

As is typical with many of the annoying phrases managers love to over-utter, *action item* suffers from both the extra, unnecessary word and the desire to make something routine sound more important.

In this case, to almost sound like a superhero.

Often, when the something is really, really, really important, it will be promoted to major *action item*.

We're talking about a task here; but, of course, "task" lacks the excitement and forward progress implications you get with *action item*. Too bad, we say.

We're well beyond the time to strike these clichés and/or cool-sounding phrases from our business vocabulary when a simple, single word will suffice. We are in the age of texting and chat; and no one is impressed by your use of *action item* when you could just say task.

Replacement phrases: Task; To do

See also: *Deliverables*

30,000-Pound Gorilla

"I know you think Frank's faking it, but I think we'll have to agree to disagree on this one."

Agree to Disagree

While saying, "We will have to *agree to disagree*" is sometimes a genuine way to move away from a contentious topic in business where both sides are making compelling points, this one is especially annoying because it's most often used by the excessively passive-aggressive in your company.

You know the type: the jerk manager who's always right; whose opinions are relayed as facts; who knows little about most topics but wants to appear as the expert on everything.

When this blockhead finds he's in an unwinnable argument, he'll never admit it. Instead, he'll *agree to disagree*.

Ugh, what a twit.

We have a better idea. How about we all agree that you're wrong? Moreover, how about we all agree that you're wrong way more often than you're right? Finally, how about we all agree that you should stop talking in meetings and try listening occasionally?

Of course, if we presented this annoying manager with these options, he'd just tell us we'll have to *agree to disagree*.

Ugh, what a twit.

Replacement phrases: No replacement needed; let's just all agree to agree this one should be stricken from everyone's vocabulary.

See also: *My Two Cents*

30,000-Pound Gorilla

Friedenthal was delighted when he finally figured out how to get all hands on deck in the office.

All Hands on Deck

While no one is truly sure why, your boss likes to sound tough. He or she likes to use phrases they've heard other tough bosses use – even if that boss was an 80-year-old Navy veteran.

Though not as annoying as sports analogies and metaphors, some military terms like *all hands on deck* continue to be overused by a few in business today. Luckily for the younger generations reading this, those who rely on these terms are likely to retire in the next decade.

Yippee, we only have to wait ten long years to stop hearing annoying jargon like *all hands on deck*!

Here's the situation: your company is facing a crisis; one that requires attention and action from more than just a couple members of the team. Your manager announces to the group, "We're going to need *all hands on deck* for this one."

Of course, the meaning is clear: we need everyone involved; everyone present; everyone focused.

After all, this is critical.

Except, of course, when we don't really need everyone involved; we don't need everyone present; we don't need everyone focused.

Make no mistake, it's almost always the case that we don't really need everyone present. We don't really need everyone focused. Because, of course, this crisis is not all that critical. In fact, it's not even a crisis.

All hands on deck is typical of most annoying phrases: the user liked the sound of it, so they latched onto it and they'll never let it go. And, because they now have it in their verbal arsenal, they use it every time they can.

Hearing this annoying phrase makes us wish we could keep our hands over our ears instead having to put them on the deck.

Replacement phrases: Full attendance; Mandatory meeting; Everyone

See also: *Boots on the Ground*

30,000-Pound Gorilla

"Sorry, Mr. Grave, your analysis paralysis doesn't qualify as a disability."

Analysis Paralysis

Analysis paralysis, unfortunately, is a very real ailment for many managers. Afraid to make a decision, the worst kinds of managers will get buried in the minutia; over-analyzing everything until they're figuratively paralyzed.

However, that's not the reason this one made the cut.

We included *analysis paralysis* in this book because like so many of these annoying phrases, managers who latch onto this one simply won't ever stop using it.

It seems whenever a decision isn't made within their timeline, your annoying boss accuses the other party of suffering from *analysis paralysis*. No facts required; simply *analysis paralysis*. If only this was the sole annoying use.

Has this ever happened to you? You create a detailed spreadsheet for your manager – something you were sure included only relevant data – and you were quickly diagnosed with *analysis paralysis*?

Never mind that your analysis was never paused, or that you failed to make a decision. Apparently, your work was just too detailed for your pea-brained manager.

Steve once worked for someone who seemed to never make decisions – that is, he genuinely suffered from *analysis paralysis* – but, and this is true for most of those who cannot make decisions, he was also the first to accuse others of overthinking everything and avoiding conclusions.

This manager's favorite annoying phrase? Nope… it was actually *herding cats*. His second favorite phrase? You guessed it! *Analysis paralysis*! Ironically doubly-annoying!

Replacement phrases: Overthinking; Overanalyzing; Caught in the minutia

See also: *Go Slow to Go Fast; Lost in the Sauce*

30,000-Pound Gorilla

Sadly, Todd never understood that saying he was going to finish a project and actually finishing a project were two different things.

Are Two Different Things

It seems nearly any two things in life and in business *are two different things*. As in, "Saying you're going to lose weight and actually doing it *are two different things*."

No crap? Are they really?

Ugh, so annoying.

This is an unnecessary phrase that must disappear. It conveys nothing but negativity and disbelief; and it's most often used by passive-aggressive managers. For example, they'll often use *are two different things* after they come out of a meeting with their boss where they "committed" to the leader's vision; albeit with a poorly-masked passive-aggressive response such as, "If that's the direction you want, we'll do everything we can to achieve it."

Later, when they gather with their cohorts, they'll express their disbelief in the vision by saying, "Well, setting his goal and actually achieving it *are two different things*."

Yeah; especially with a schmuck like you working for him!

Certainly, there are an infinite number of pairs of things that *are two different things*; yet this phrase is only used when the differences are obvious. This, of course, makes it doubly-annoying.

Indeed, saying something and actually doing that something *are two different things*. They are always two different things! Always!

How about committing now to stop using this annoying phrase?

Of course, saying you're going to stop saying it and actually no longer saying it *are two different things*, aren't they?

Replacement phrases: No replacement needed – just stop already!

See also: *Easier Said Than Done; It Is What It Is*

30,000-Pound Gorilla

"If our SMEs can't grow the YOY and YTD ROI on our B2C business ASAP, we're going to struggle to make payroll by EOW."

ASAP

Let's *level set* for a moment: (yes, you caught us, *level set* is an annoying phrase managers overuse – that's why it's in italics) *ASAP* is an acronym that simply means "as soon as possible." It's often shortened to *ASAP* (pronounced ey-sap) because the very nature of the request means even the request itself must be spewed forth as quickly as any human on earth could ever say it.

"I need this *ASAP*," is certainly more efficient (and impolite) than saying, "I need this completed as soon as possible, please."

The problem with *ASAP* – and why it's so annoying – is the extra emphasis on immediacy that's implied when one uses *ASAP* instead of something like "right away" or "as soon as possible."

The *ASAP* request – to the requestor – is infinitely more important than a request for something "as soon as possible." Of course, the pinnacle of annoying with this acronym is the occasional moronic manager whose request is so urgent that he needs something A-S-A-P. Taking the extra time to announce each letter separately most certainly means that his request ranks even higher in importance to any merely needed *ASAP*.

By the way, if you find yourself with a boss who overuses *ASAP*, and you'd like to find a way to keep from cringing each time he utters it, just separate the acronym into two words in your mind. Just imagine he signed his request as "a sap." So, instead of hearing, "I need this *ASAP*," you'll hear, "I need this, (signed) A Sap."

You're welcome.

Replacement phrases: As soon as possible; Right away; Immediately

See also: *FYI*

Why McKinley Failed His Millennial Boss

Ask, The

Almost no phrase in this book makes the pompous pricks at work sound more like pompous pricks than when they refer to a deadline or a request as *the ask*.

For example, "*The ask* was for all *deliverables* to be decided by Friday, so we could *hit the ground running* Monday morning." (As you can tell, those who use *the ask* will invariably use additional annoying phrases in the same sentence to prove their pomposity.)

While the word "ask" can be considered an informal noun for the British (allowing you to put "the" in front of it, as one might when describing a noun), using *the ask* as some managers do today… in business… in America is reserved just for the too-cool-for-school crowd among us.

Not to pick on any one demographic, but we've never heard a Baby Boomer use this term; only Millennials.

Coincidence? Not likely. When you mean request, say request. When you mean deadline, say deadline.

For example, "The request was for all tasks to be decided by Friday, so the team is ready Monday morning." Same meaning, less prickishness.

Replacement phrases: Request; Deadline

See also: *Tear Down, The*

30,000-Pound Gorilla

"If we want our department to appear competent in this meeting, I need Wilkinson to constantly overstate the obvious; and Malone, I need you to start every sentence with 'at the end of the day'."

At the End of the Day

Using *at the end of the day* wouldn't be a problem, if *at the end of the day* ever actually referred to 5:00 p.m., or midnight, or whenever your day officially ends.

Of course, as anyone in business knows, *at the end of the day* never means at the end of today or at closing time. Most often it's used to mean "when all the evidence/information has been gathered and reviewed," as in, "*At the end of the day*, I'm hopeful you'll see it as we do."

Additionally, *at the end of the day* is sometimes used to refer to the completion of some project – though, most often a project that takes much longer than a single day to complete.

Finally, *at the end of the day* is often used as a simple, wholly unnecessary filler. In these cases, of course, just removing the phrase completely will convey your meaning more clearly than adding *at the end of the day*. For example, as in this exchange:

> "Are you looking at any other possible joint ventures in the industry?"
>
> "*At the end of the day*, we're interested in anything that can show a positive ROI."

Now, try that response without *at the end of the day*. Clearer meaning; no annoyance.

On a side note: as much as managers overuse this phrase, it seems no athlete or coach can answer a reporter's question without inserting *at the end of the day* in their response.

"*At the end of the day*, this team played their hearts out."

Maddening that we cannot escape this annoying phrase even when sitting at home in front of the television.

Replacement phrases: When we/you have all the information; When it's completed. Most often, of course, there is no replacement needed – just stop saying it.

See also: *That Said; So*

"The boss did say to meet at this juncture, didn't he?"

At This Juncture/At This Point in Time

The long-winded, loquacious nature of these two overly-wordy phrases are simply nothing more than verbosity at its finest – so much so they both do indeed border on the periphrastic. (Yes, we used a thesaurus to write that sentence!)

But seriously, when you intend to mean "now," why not just say "now?" If you feel the word "now" needs some sort of extra emphasis, you can always go with "right now" … right? *At this juncture* and *at this point in time* are just filler used by those managers who subscribe to the "More is More" philosophy of communication.

These guys and gals love to hear themselves speak so much they include as many words as possible to describe everything. They're the ones who hold the longest meetings that resolve the fewest number of issues. They're also the ones you and your coworkers strive to avoid in the hallways and common spaces of your office.

Of course, because they're clueless, they interpret your standoffishness as merely a lack of understanding just how important they are… so, they're inclined to provide you even more useless information the next time you interact. Ugh.

Replacement phrases: Now; Currently

See also: *Currently Now*

30,000-Pound Gorilla

For the twelfth consecutive year, the Clarksville Ugly Baby Contest had no entries.

Baby is Ugly

For some reason, annoying managers (and especially annoying consultants) feel the need to explain their (self-perceived) unique level of honesty in a way that's insulting to ugly babies worldwide.

They'll proclaim to everyone who will listen that they're not afraid to tell a client their *baby is ugly*.

Bravo. Brav-freakin-oh! (To be clear, we know "annoying consultants" is redundant - we wrote it that way for effect.)

When someone boasts they're willing to tell a client when their *baby is ugly*, please just punch them right in the mouth. No babies are ugly. Except, of course, the ugly ones. Therefore, no one – especially a parent – wants to hear about an ugly baby.

Life, you might find surprising, is not like an episode of *Seinfeld* – you're almost never involved in a conversation about ugly babies. Given this, can we just stop creating false bravado and drop this annoying phrase from the business lexicon?

Replacement phrases: Tell the truth; Be honest

See also: *Warts and All*

30,000-Pound Gorilla

Despite their best efforts, the team always found themselves back to square one.

Back to Square One

Hearing *back to square one* begs the question: What games do our annoying managers think we're playing?

Snakes and Ladders? Chutes and Ladders? Four Square? Hopscotch?

We know what this irritating supervisor means when we hear, "Attention everyone! We're going *back to square one*," but this doesn't make it any less annoying.

Yes, we're starting over, we get it. Now, can we just have a boss who regurgitates fewer childhood idioms and instead speaks like an educated adult?

We suppose what makes this one especially annoying is the satisfying way many managers use *back to square one*. Is it just us, or do many of them seem pleased that we failed? Like those who revel in the misfortunes of the rich and famous, the business world is filled with managers who secretly wish for failure – even among their own teams.

They root for failure… that is, unless it's their project or their idea. Interestingly, there's a word for those who take pleasure in the pain of others; it's the German word Schadenfreude (literally, harm + joy).

Of course, just because there's a word for it doesn't mean it's okay, right?

There's a word for killing someone, yet that doesn't make murder okay – even if it's your annoying manager we're speaking about.

The only pleasure anyone in your workplace should get from another's pain is if that annoying manager even contracted laryngitis.

Schadenfreude indeed!

Replacement phrases: Start over; Regroup

See also: *Back to the Drawing Board*

Because of Wassmann's overuse of annoying business phrases, the entire team turned their backs to the drawing board in one last great act of defiance.

Back to the Drawing Board

In today's workplace, no one is still using a drawing board, are they? In this case, saying, "Back to the whiteboard" might be more appropriate if it wasn't also annoying.

Like *back to square one*, *back to the drawing board* is often an attempt to revel in the misfortunes of others. In some perverse cases, this can also be the office equivalent of Munchausen by proxy. Your boss sees himself as the savior of the team – and he can only be the savior if the rest of you are in need of saving.

If this is how most annoying managers use *back to the drawing board* – he or she has a sickness; one that no encyclopedia of annoying phrases is going to cure.

However, *back to the drawing board* is also ancient; and likely confusing to Millennial and Gen Z employees. While it's been a few years since either of us remembers hearing *back to the drawing board*, friends report differently.

It seems many managers – those frustrated with their team's progress – still (almost proudly) announce, "It's time to go *back to the drawing board*."

Ugh, truly annoying.

Of course, *back to the drawing board* implies completely starting over… from the very beginning… with a blank canvas, if you will. This, even if the issue is merely a roadblock or hiccup. The reality is project roadblocks and hiccups are common, and if we went *back to the drawing board* each time we faced some adverse condition, we'd never accomplish anything at work.

Instead of going *back to the drawing board*, what if we just solved the current issue and moved ahead? Now there's a novel concept.

Of course, since merely solving a minor issue and moving ahead is missing the drama associated with scrapping everything and starting over, your annoying boss won't be able to enjoy that satisfied feeling he gets by declaring the efforts to this point as wasted.

Poor guy.

Replacement phrases: Start over

See also: *Back to Square One*

"I'm in the ballpark... where are you?"

Ballpark

While certainly not the most annoying sports phrase used in business, one specific iteration of *ballpark* is downright maddening.

The pretentious request from above for you to "*ballpark* me something" makes us cringe. *Ballpark*, in this example, is no longer a noun: it's a verb. An ear-bleeding misuse uttered only to make the speaker sound hip.

To be clear, when you ask someone to *ballpark* you something, you sound like a boob; a boob no one wants to work very hard for.

If you need your team to provide you with estimates, ask them to provide you with estimates. If you insist on using *ballpark* in these requests, at least use it correctly. As in, "Can you provide me a *ballpark*?"

Using *ballpark* as a noun to describe proximity or estimate was the initial and correct adoption of this word. Explaining that someone is close (perhaps during a negotiation) to what you're thinking by letting them know they're "in the *ballpark*" seems like a fine use to us.

It's appropriate and not that annoying – at least not to us. Of course, like most everyone else in the workplace, we could be persuaded to ban *ballpark* and every other sports term and analogy, and not lose any sleep over it.

Replacement phrases: Estimate; Close

See also: *Wheelhouse; Bullet-Point Me Something*

30,000-Pound Gorilla

"I don't think Scarbrough has the bandwidth for this new promotion."

Bandwidth

Bandwidth originated from the telecommunications and broadcasting fields, where it (basically) describes the range of frequencies within a band – the width of a given band. (Save your letters of outrage if you're a ham radio operator. This definition is not meant to help someone pass their geek certification.)

In business, *bandwidth* can be used to describe one's physical ability to handle additional tasks and/or their mental capacity (or even intelligence). As in, "Fred is really swamped; I don't think he has the *bandwidth* to tackle an additional project right now."

On the surface, this might seem like a fairly accurate expression; one that's properly used in most situations.

If only.

Our problem we have with the way *bandwidth* is used by managers is in its overuse. Those who say it, say it dozens of times a day. They use it to describe everything from how the office copier performs to their ability to love another human being.

Moreover, it's impossible to get through a meeting about anything these days without hearing it at least once. Add a *bandwidth* aficionado to your meeting and it will be the only word you remember from the entire 90 minutes you'll never get back in your life.

Finally, this one becomes extra annoying when it's used as an insult – as it most often is in the workplace. Irritating managers almost never applaud someone's *bandwidth*, as in, "She's really got a lot of *bandwidth*." However, these same bosses are quick to point out someone's shortcomings with, "Yeah, he just doesn't have the *bandwidth* for this project."

To these simpletons we say, "Get a mirror."

Replacement phrases: Ability; Capacity

See also: *Download*

As punishment for a bad audit, the CEO sent the accounting team into the field for some remedial training.

Bean Counter

We bet you're wondering where the term *bean counter* originated, right?

Well, if that's the case, go look on the internet because we don't care where it came from, only that everyone stop using this silly, outdated, and often derogatory designation when referring to our accounting teams.

Not that either of us has a great deal of positive feelings for accountants – we're truly ambivalent when it comes to these folks.

Accountants have a clearly defined role; one that when accomplished correctly leads to zero drama or issues. Accountants are sort of like the tires on your car. That is, so long as they're working as designed, we pay them no attention.

It's only when they fail that we notice tires or accountants.

We understand the term *bean counter* most often refers to those pesky accountants who put the numbers above all else – including sales and profits. The annoying folks in your company call them *bean counters* to dismiss or diminish their advice.

They do this because they're unhappy someone on the accounting team chose the safe route over their risky idea.

Our issue with *bean counter* being used today is not the negative connotation; rather, the annoyance comes from the century in which we're living today.

Look at the calendar on your iPhone! It's the 21st Century, dammit!

If you find yourself uttering *bean counter* today, we insist you also start saying "fiddle-faddle" or "horse feathers" when describing anything nonsensical. At least this way you'll be using the proper vernacular as you skedaddle off to the speakeasy to get zozzled on a Gin Rickey.

Now that would be the cat's meow!

Replacement phrases: Accountant; CFO; Controller; Accounting Team

See also: *Headhunter*

30,000-Pound Gorilla

"Well, it looks like you can beat a dead horse after all."

Beat a Dead Horse

In the politically-correct world we live – one where every word you use can get twisted by social justice warriors – it seems this saying might get you into trouble with your local PETA chapter.

Although we never seem to find ourselves jumping into the "cancel culture" mentality, *beat a dead horse* is more than outdated and annoying; it's morbid. Moreover, it conjures up an image that's cruel and disgusting.

We understand the user is not genuinely trying to build a picture in your mind of someone repeatedly striking a deceased equine – they're not cruel and disgusting, just oblivious to the words and phrases spewing from that hole below their nose.

If you feel it's okay to warn someone, "Let's not *beat a dead horse*," you should realize you're telling them it's fine to beat a live horse.

Can we agree that anyone beating live horses is a sadistic freak deserving of the harshest punishment available by law? Great; now let's figure out what the annoying manager using this phrase really means.

Beat a dead horse is most often used to tell someone they should stop repeating the same request, complaint, mantra, question, or opinion. That is, the horse you were trying to kill with your club is now dead; therefore, you can stop beating it. The additional blows to the carcass are redundant.

Simply put, your message/proposal/question has been heard; it's been ignored or rejected; move on.

Replacement phrases: Stop; Move on

See also: *Drink/Drank the Kool-Aid*

30,000-Pound Gorilla

"I'm afraid under 'Experience' we're going to require a little more than 'Been There, Done That'."

Been There, Done That

When a manager or coworker annoyingly tells you they've *been there, done that*, they're explaining in the most irritating terms that whatever the task, issue, or opportunity ahead, it borders on tedium for them.

After all, they've *been there, done that*, right?

They're more than experienced; they've seen it all. In fact, you're a nuisance for even bringing it up. Shame on you. Don't you understand the genius you're working with? Don't you appreciate the vast knowledge and skill in front of you?

Of course, those that reach for this tired phrase are among the most annoying people who will ever occupy a seat in your workplace. Likewise, they're the most exhausting windbags you will ever work with or work for.

If their only transgression was their near daily *been there, done that*, we could forgive them and move on. No, they are the masters of the clichéd; the hackneyed; the worn-out.

They dip into the trough of annoying phrases like it's the sundae bar at Golden Corral – they want to get all they can right now in case the world explodes, and the restaurant manager is forced to shut down the soft serve machine.

They spew annoying phrases because they can… and because they're oblivious to everyone's (correct) perception of them.

Clearly, they're mostly right. It seems they've *been there, done that* (again and again) when it comes to annoying jargon.

Replacement phrases: Experienced (or, perhaps just stop saying telling everyone how smart or experienced you are and see if your sentences sound less douchey)

See also: *Not My First Rodeo*

30,000-Pound Gorilla

"Geez, everywhere we go it seems we're behind the eight ball."

48

Behind the Eight Ball

Like many of the annoying phrases managers have over-uttered over the last century, *behind the eight ball* finds its origins in a game. In this case, billiards.

When the eight ball (that black one with the number 8 on it) sits between the cue ball (that white one you strike when playing pool) and the ball you wish to hit with the cue ball, you are quite literally *behind the eight ball*. In other words, you're in a bad situation, as you have no easy shot.

It's cliché enough to use this one correctly; though unfortunately, many managers insist on claiming they are *behind the eight ball* when they simply mean they have a tight deadline, a full schedule, or are facing a tough sale.

"Boy, we are really *behind the eight ball* on the Kershner account!"

No, you're not. You are trailing; your firm is not in first place; your competition, Snyder, has a better chance of landing the Kershner account than you do. You are not *behind the eight ball*… you're just behind.

Therefore, given that you can't even use a cliché correctly, just stop saying it. Instead, try describing the situation as it really is.

"Boy, winning the Kershner account is going to require more preparation and a better presentation from us."

Doesn't that sound better? At least this way the team understands what is required to win the account instead of all the Millennials on your staff wondering why you sound like their grandpa.

Replacement phrases: Disadvantaged; Out of options; On a deadline

See also: *Between a Rock and a Hard Place*

30,000-Pound Gorilla

"It's the best thing since sliced bread. We call it sliced mustard."

Best Thing Since Sliced Bread

While the automatic slicing of bread has only been around commercially for less than a century, there have certainly been more than a few inventions and innovations of greater note since retailers began offering loaves in slices.

To say something is the *best thing since sliced bread* is to poopoo these superior accomplishments. It shows you're not only an annoying manager, but that you're also delusional. Sliced bread is a good thing, but as an innovation, it pales in comparison to so many others that have come since its broad acceptance.

The electron microscope, ballpoint pens, VCRs, helicopters, the Internet, personal computers, mobile phones, the McRib, and Coke Zero all come to mind.

To say something is the *best thing since sliced bread* implies sliced bread is a greater innovation than the McRib or Coke Zero. On this point, we must object.

When your annoying manager tells you something is the *best thing since sliced bread*, ask him or her what century this is. Then, take a sip of your Coke Zero (strangely called Coke Zero Sugar now because, apparently, diet pop drinkers couldn't comprehend what the Zero meant), let out a long, an audible "ahhhh" and smile knowing there have been hundreds of superior innovations since we started slicing bread —that can in your hand is proof of this. (And proof your manager is an idiot.)

Replacement phrases: Great idea

See also: *Reinvent the Wheel*

Nelson never could get over being put between Rock and Hardplace.

Between a Rock and a Hard Place

This is the worst idiom of all time – at least on the annoying scale – often describing when someone or some group is faced with only two distasteful decisions; or (less often) has placed themselves into a truly bad situation.

They are said to be *between a rock and a hard place*.

They're where? Between a rock and another rock? We're sorry, but we never quite got this one. To us, this saying never implied some sort of *Sophie's Choice* – a truly difficult decision where all outcomes royally suck.

Today, it's mostly hyperbole, isn't it? When your annoying boss describes the company's situation as being *between a rock and a hard place*, he's being overly dramatic. Virtually no decisions in the workplace today come down to two choices where each is equally distasteful. One is almost always preferable – making the choice easy.

This idiom becomes especially annoying when neither choice is a rock or a hard place. This occurs when you work for one of those dolts afraid to make decisions. They wrongly believe that all choices have equally bad consequences, so they make no decision.

Of course, no decision is virtually always the worst decision of all – often putting the company where?

Yep, *between a rock and a hard place*.

Replacement phrases: Difficult decision; Bad situation

See also: *Behind the Eight Ball*

Like everything in his life, Clyde liked to adhere to the literal meaning of bio break.

Bio Break

The term *bio break* is annoying on many levels; although, not the least of which is the snarkiness by which it's usually delivered.

Interestingly, even more annoying is this: While *bio break* is meant to be a clever way to say "potty break" without making people think of actual poop and pee, adding the word "bio" makes us (and others) think of biohazard. Consequently, this unfortunately conjures up images of a massive poop accident – a shitstorm, if you will; something only men in yellow, hermetically-sealed suits can contain.

Certainly, the use of this annoying phrase began as a clever way to discuss the need for attendees at a meeting or conference to use the restroom for something other than resting.

My goodness, are we expected to actually say the words "bathroom break" in today's day and age?

How gauche.

Just the thought of having to express to a crowd of people that we understand they are humans; that humans eat and drink; that because of this behavior, they occasionally must poop and pee is distasteful.

Moreover, since we don't want the attendees pooping and peeing all over themselves, we need to afford them some sort of brief reprieve from the meeting so they will have the time necessary to poop and pee in a proper place.

But, you see, we can't bring ourselves to make these acknowledgements. Therefore, we announce in a sardonic, cooler-than-thou tone, "We'll have a *bio break* at the top of the hour."

Gosh, don't we seem like just the hippest managers ever!

Replacement phrases: Break

See also: *Shit Where You Eat*

30,000-Pound Gorilla

"Clearly, Dowdy's department is just better at the blocking and tackling."

Blocking and Tackling

Generally, when someone or some team in your workplace skips the basics and fails, managers will often say "it's just *blocking and tackling.*" This, to indicate the simplest of tasks were not completed.

While most everyone knows this saying denotes the essential tasks in (North American) football, the most annoying among your managers may argue it refers to a block and tackle system of pulleys and ropes used to lift heavy loads.

That's just idiotic overthinking, of course. No one in North America today hears the term *blocking and tackling* and thinks of anything other than football players executing the basics.

Of course, we find this phrase to be the most annoying of all the overused sports analogies applied to business because it implies that *blocking and tackling* are easy, basic tasks.

In American football, we'll argue, *blocking and tackling* are the most important tasks assigned to anyone on the team; and certainly not the easiest.

Without blocking, the offense cannot score. Without tackling, the defense cannot stop the offense.

Since we don't actually block or tackle at work (unless you do employ pulleys and ropes to lift things), let's drop this silly, annoying misuse.

Replacement phrases: The basics

See also: *It's not Rocket Science/It's not Brain Surgery*

"Well, Yamaura said he wanted more boots on the ground, though I'm not sure how that's going to help us grow profits this quarter."

Boots on the Ground

Uncreative managers – especially those who never served in the armed forces – seem to gravitate toward tough-sounding, military replacement phrases for the most mundane things. From calling a training seminar a "boot camp" to referring to their meeting space as "the war room;" some managers try too hard to make the mundane seem important; almost dangerous.

This spills over into staffing when they discuss the need for additional employees in the field. As in, "We need more *boots on the ground.*"

How tough you are Mr. Manager! It's a war out there, isn't it? If you're going to win this war, you've got to have those *boots on the ground*, right?

Wait, you're not letting the title General Manager go to your head, are you? You do understand you're not really a General, right?

If we really want to get technical (and overly-PC) about this annoying use of military jargon in business, we could take offense to the boots portion of the phrase.

Is your manager advocating for only men to tackle this daring role? Or, perhaps, since most businessmen don't wear boots, while many businesswomen do, perhaps your manager is really an enlightened leader looking to bring more women into your company's field force.

Of course, neither scenario is likely. Managers using this phrase are most often dullards of the self-important variety. They don't think beyond the superficial veneer on any subject… they're just trying to sound tough.

Replacement phrases: Field teams; Staffing; Headcount

See also: *All Hands on Deck; Troops*

30,000-Pound Gorilla

"I'm pretty sure we've identified the bottleneck."

Bottleneck

To be clear, saying *bottleneck* is fine when you mean *bottleneck*. That is, when you're referring to a step in a process where progress is obstructed.

Bottleneck, you see, correctly refers to a restricted flow, if you will. It does not, however, mean every hindrance, hurdle, or obstruction you encounter on your path to your goals.

This phrase is only annoying when used incorrectly. Unfortunately, in the business world, it's nearly always used incorrectly.

If you're designing workflows through multiple stations – let's say in a factory – and one station is holding up the flow of goods because they cannot produce their portion of the project at the same speed as the other stations; you have a legitimate *bottleneck*.

Conversely, if you have a salesman who is underperforming; you have an underperforming salesman. Please slap yourself in the face if you find yourself describing this salesman as a *bottleneck*, as in, "We'd hit our number if only Tyler wasn't such a *bottleneck*."

The only *bottleneck* in this instance is your own neck. It's limiting the blood flow to your brain. Add a dictionary app to your smartphone and start using it. This may help you sound less foolish in business situations.

Replacement phrases: Obstruction; Hindrance; Issue

See also: *Behind the Eight Ball*

30,000-Pound Gorilla

"The bottom line is we've crossed the bottom line."

Bottom Line

If we're talking about net profit, then we have no problem with referencing the *bottom line*.

Of course, when you're annoying managers speak about the *bottom line*, they're really just talking about some important point… or the essential element of a deal… or the expected outcome of a project… or a myriad of other things wholly unrelated to the true *bottom line*.

So, so annoying.

Look, the *bottom line* on this annoying expression is that it's unnecessarily dramatic. The *bottom line* is you don't need to constantly refer to the *bottom line* when you're really just trying to make a point. The *bottom line* is that people will respect you more if you simply stop beginning every sentence with "the *bottom line* is… ."

The *bottom line* is this can get very annoying… very annoying. Can't it?

We think we made our point.

Replacement phrases: Important point; Essential element; Expected outcome

See also: *Total-Total*

"No one was more prepared than Ebersole to always bring their 'A' game."

Bring Your 'A' Game

Ugh, another sports analogy brought into the business world!

Of course, the worst part of this annoying phrase is those who utter it assume their subordinates often show up with their 'B' or 'C' games. Should we infer their team is made up primarily of slackers who will give their best only when pressed?

If that's the case – to keep the sports analogies going – this sounds like a coaching issue… and not a problem with the players.

To be clear, there are going to be situations in your business – perhaps once a year or so for most teams – where the outcome is so critical everyone needs to be reminded of its significance. In these cases, we prefer to speak without clichés and merely ensure everyone understands (in plain language) the importance of a positive outcome.

If you're one who must regularly and openly ask the most from your team, perhaps instead of reminding them they need to bring a given "game" via your tired clichés, you should work to develop your leadership skills until everyone is giving their best all the time.

You know, bringing it *24/7/365* like you do, right?

Replacement phrases: Arrive prepared; Be ready; Do your best

See also: *Give 110%; Work Smarter, Not Harder; 24/7/365*

30,000-Pound Gorilla

Sadly, Nenni was unable to bubble up his sales numbers.

Bubble It Up

Somehow, it's no longer enough to demonstrate or share in your workplace. Today, your annoying managers want to be sure you *bubble it up*.

Do what?

While this one always makes us cringe, it also makes us wonder how exactly one bubbles something up? Is this a natural process or do we need to exert some force below the topic, project, or whatever it is we're supposed to be bubbling up?

If we *bubble it up*, will this be sufficient? Will this be enough to ensure a successful completion? Or, will we also need to check for receipt and understanding? Will we need to inspect the follow-through? Will we need to actually understand what *bubble it up* means?

Bubble it up is annoying on the surface and especially in its ambiguity. It's used by the weakest of annoying managers; those too afraid to truly lead. It comes out as a suggestion because, well, a clear order might create some conflict.

Asking someone to *bubble it up* is akin to asking them if they wouldn't mind wearing pants around the office.

It's weak… and everyone but you knows it.

Replacement phrases: Show; Share; Demonstrate

See also: *Cascade; Waterfall*

30,000-Pound Gorilla

"Leo, baby. This stuff is great, but can't you just bullet-point me something?"

Bullet-Point Me Something

This annoying phrase is gaining popularity with managers suffering from self-inflicted attention deficit disorders.

Screen addiction is real and pervasive; and with so many managers constantly checking their smartphones – playing games, checking scores, tallying their social media likes – they find they cannot concentrate on anything long enough to be bothered to read actual paragraphs. (That's one of the reasons this book and one of Steve's other books, *Sh*t Sandwich*, employ short chapters and cartoons to get the points across to today's audience.)

Many of today's managers, unfortunately, find they can only handle quick bullet points – usually presented in an outline – regardless of how important or in-depth your analysis of a subject should be.

They can't even bother to read the *Cliff Notes*; they just want the bullet points. Of course, this means you're required to take any great idea and extract only the "relevant" themes and present these in simple, easy-to-read, quick blurbs when you manager insists you *bullet-point me something*.

Short of curing your manager of her screen addiction, you're left with explaining *War and Peace* as a "big book about Russia in the early 1800s."

Of course, for most distracted managers, this synopsis is still likely too long for someone wanting you to just *bullet-point me something*.

Analysis aside, we, like many of you, find *bullet-point me something* simply annoying. Especially when what the requestor really wants is a brief analysis.

Replacement phrases: Brief me; Give me a brief analysis

See also: *Ballpark*

30,000-Pound Gorilla

"My orders were to burn the boats AFTER we landed in the New World!"

Burn the Boats

This annoying phrase originates from the ancient practice of a ship captain (after landing in some new territory) forcing his crew to conquer the enemy (in the case of Cortez scuttling his ships when he landed in Mexico) or to make the most of a difficult transition (in the case of the Bounty mutineers burning their ship when they landed on Pitcarin Island).

The idea is that you *burn the boats* to remove any opportunity for retreat. This way, your crewmembers are compelled to use every (remaining) available resource to survive.

For your crew at work, your manager commands you to *burn the boats* to ensure you're committed to the goal.

An example of this might be when a new process is introduced where the manager is fearful that the team may resort to using the old process at the first sign of discomfort. A commendable strategy for sure, though one that deserves a better appellation… perhaps one from this millennium… perhaps one that's not so annoying.

Replacement phrases: Commit

See also: *Buy-In*

30,000-Pound Gorilla

"LaPorte wanted to agree with his boss, but he just couldn't afford the buy-in."

Buy-In

One of the most annoying aspects of the overuse of *buy-in* – as in, "Do we have your *buy-in*?" – is that the person asking this question only wants to know if you agree with them; they're not looking for a monetary commitment of any kind.

It's a complete misuse of the term!

The actual definition of *buy-in* (or simply "buy in" without the hyphen) includes some payment for some share of a possession or right. In other words, *buy-in* is a full-on commitment that most often includes an exchange of funds.

When your typical manager asks for your *buy-in*, they're just checking to see if you like the new overtime policy or where they decided to move the coffee maker. Hardly situations where more than a simple agreement is required.

If you're looking for an agreement, ask for an agreement. If you seek a commitment, ask for a commitment. When you ask for someone's *buy-in*, you think you sound like a savvy businessperson, while the rest of us know you're just a dolt.

Replacement phrases: Agreement; Commitment

See also: *Burn the Boats; Hammer it Out*

It looks like IT is finally cascading the new technology down to HR."

Cascade

One would guess *cascade* sounds like it's the opposite of *bubble it up*. Interestingly, in your workplace it means the same thing. *Cascade* just indicates a different direction – of course, it's just as annoying.

Cascade is interchangeable with *bubble it up*, though it's rare any annoying manager is using both.

Annoying managers, you see, usually pick their favorite five or fifty-five or five hundred fifty-five annoying phrases to latch onto, and then they never let go… never… ever.

In fact, it might be refreshing (and certainly less annoying) if your manager occasionally mixed it up a bit and substituted one painful term for another. We're certainly never going to succeed in getting them to stop altogether with the annoying vernacular, right?

Cascade most often replaces "share;" which, apparently is too boring to say aloud.

"Barb, please share this with the team," is clearly yawnsville for the annoying people at your company. Instead, they'll only feel self-satisfied if they ask you to *cascade* something to your team.

"Barb, I need you to *cascade* this to the team."

Ugh.

The only thing we'd like to *cascade* after hearing this is the guy who said it… *cascade* him right out the door.

If only.

Replacement phrases: Show; Share; Demonstrate

See also: *Bubble it Up; Waterfall*

30,000-Pound Gorilla

"Well, you certainly have experience as a change agent..."

Change Agent

Change agent is both annoying and confusing; though, the annoyance factor for this one is tripled when someone describes themselves as a *change agent*.

In fact, if *change agent* was only used when complimenting someone else or when providing a recruiter with the type of individual you want them to find, it might not even be all that annoying.

But, alas, those who like to talk about how they're *crushing it* while they *hustle* and *grind* will often let you know they're also a *change agent* (not to mention a ninja, *guru* or industry *thought leader* – or all of the above!).

Like all things in life, when you find the end zone, act as if you've been there before.

For the *change agents* reading this: stop calling yourself a *change agent*. Just be one… the rest of us will figure it out.

By the way, the rest of us need to shun anyone who calls themselves a *change agent*, just as we would anyone who gives themselves a nickname. It's pathetic behavior that should not be encouraged.

If you're tempted to call someone else a *change agent*, find a more descriptive word like effective, skilled, talented, or productive; and then follow this with something like "leader."

We'll all be better off in the long run.

Replacement phrases: Effective

See also: *Disruptor; Thought Leader*

30,000-Pound Gorilla

"When I said we needed someone with cat-like reflexes, this isn't what I meant."

Chasing Shiny Objects

We'll admit it. Steve has overused this phrase from time to time. In his defense, of course, he felt *chasing shiny objects* best described what he was trying to convey at the time.

That's the problem with every phrase in this book: the user believes their use of an annoying cliché is justified. Moreover, they don't believe the phrases they use to be annoying; just descriptive and necessary.

Often, they're neither… and Steve can now admit this. You see, he is a recovering cliché-aholic.

Chasing shiny objects is most often meant as an insult to describe the efforts of some entity that doesn't understand what drives growth in their industry. They are said to be *chasing shiny objects* (instead of focusing on the important, often boring tasks and solutions).

Many people in consumer-facing industries saw good examples of this during the Pokémon Go craze of 2016-2017. We witnessed car dealerships, realtors, and even plumbing companies devising strategies, expending labor, and spending real money trying to lure their share of Pokémon Go players (heads buried in their phones) to their establishments.

Guess what? For many of these companies it worked! Some businesses were mobbed by hordes of zombies throwing imaginary Poké Balls as they attempted to catch some elusive (and valuable?) Pokémon.

If you owned a restaurant, café or bar, this might have been a good strategy. If you're a car dealer, real estate agent, or plumber, you saw your parking lot crowded with Millennials who bought nothing; though likely cost you business simply by taking up space.

You, it could be said, were *chasing shiny objects*. Of course, since we won't be using this term any longer, we will just say you were unfocused – even if Steve slips, and accuses you of *chasing shiny objects*.

Like we wrote, Steve's recovering… not cured.

Replacement phrases: Unfocused

See also: *Reinvent the Wheel*

30,000-Pound Gorilla

"Next week, be sure to circle back... oh, never mind."

Circle Back

A circle, of course, is a circle. This means that if you're going to *circle back* to something, you're going to be right here... where you are right now... where you started your circle... back, right?

We understand when a manager asks someone to *circle back*, they mean to get back to them at some later date with some additional information. *Circle back*, then, does actually mean to come back to here; to *circle back*. This doesn't mean it's not annoying... or sometimes misused.

The best example of misuse is when the speaker simply intends to follow up. Certainly, you've experienced salespeople tell you they're going to *circle back* with you, even though they don't plan to gather more information in the meantime. They just failed to close you today, so they're going to waste more of your time next week.

Circle back is used correctly when someone is going to move forward in a project or process, gather new information, and then come back (or *circle back*) to you with their findings. Unfortunately, those prone to use *circle back* begin to create *circle back* situations for everything.

We're torn whether it's the overuse or misuse of *circle back* that is the most annoying, so we're not going to guess. We're just going to declare it annoying and leave it at that.

Replacement phrases: Follow up; Get back in touch; Meet later

See also: *Connect With*

30,000-Pound Gorilla

"Well, it looks like you finally got them to do something as a team."

Circular Firing Squad

The ultimate in self-destruction by a group, a *circular firing squad* indicates a situation where everyone (who should be aligned) is firing at their comrades.

More specifically, they're engaging in infighting and other internal disputes; while the goal should be to direct their destruction at the enemy – that is, the competition.

To be clear, we've experienced our share of team dissention, but never thought of describing it as a *circular firing squad*. Those who use this term are prone to hyperbole, and likely should simply stop reaching for clichés and euphemisms, and just tell us what the hell they're really trying to say.

Over-using *circular firing squad*, not surprisingly, has a clear correlation to inferior leadership.

Those who reach for this term demonstrate to the rest of us they're not very good at managing people. Whether there truly is team-wide dissention of they're just trying to get two of their subordinates to come together on an issue, a real leader would handle the dispute without the need to label it with a cliché.

Moreover, a real leader wouldn't have these issues in the first place.

Replacement phrases: No replacement phrase needed; just handle the issues as they occur. (You know, be a leader?)

See also: *Silos*

30,000-Pound Gorilla

"I think Webb is taking the whole client engagement thing a bit too far."

Client Engagement

We're confused. If you're trying to increase your *client engagement*, does this mean you're in search of a fiancé? If so, do you expect to start picking out china patterns and registering at Macy's at some point?

Though *client engagement* might be correct terminology to describe the interaction between your team and your customer, it's still quite annoying to those who are forced to hear you say it repeatedly.

Client engagement is not wrong, per se, it's just overused by the most pompous of managers. If you're describing, for example, multiple touchpoints in your relationship with a customer or prospect, then the all-inclusive *client engagement* is appropriate.

However – and this is where hearing it uttered becomes annoying – if your manager is describing a specific act of communication (like a phone call or an in-person visit or even just an email), you don't want to hear, "It's important for you to increase your level of *client engagement* this quarter."

In its place, a simple, "You need to make more sales calls" conveys the message more clearly and includes the accountability that goes missing when managers try being overly verbose.

Think about it, one could argue they've increased *client engagement* when they've accomplished nothing more than sending a mass email or placing a targeted ad on Facebook. There's generally no personal accountability in those acts (beyond hitting send or creating the ad). There's also little actual engagement occurring.

Our annoyance with this term is only compounded by those smug organizations that insist on bestowing *client engagement* as a title on someone lucky enough to have a job that never has to show a return; as in Director of *Client Engagement*.

Ugh. Is there a douchier job title one could bestow on another human being? We think not. Our apologies if that's your title.

Unless you're a self-important, attention-seeking twit, we would ask for a change.

Replacement phrases: Client communication; Phone call; Email

See also: *Touch Base; Ping*

30,000-Pound Gorilla

"Why didn't someone come to me with this problem sooner?"

Come to Jesus Meeting

Despite the name of this meeting, there really is nothing Christian (or even religious) about it.

This hackneyed, overused phrase is meant to show that the speaker is not just serious or even really serious this time; but, rather, he or she is really, really, really serious! So serious, in fact, that, "If Bob doesn't step up his performance, we're going to have a *Come to Jesus Meeting*!"

It's meant to convey the importance (and maybe the overdue nature) of a meeting where a supervisor is going to finally lay down the law or where a crisis is finally going to be addressed.

The saying is annoying on many levels; but to us, it's mostly annoying because a meeting with Jesus (even if you're an atheist) sounds pretty cool, doesn't it?

Think about it: if you could meet anyone from history, wouldn't someone known as the Son of God be near the top of most everyone's list? How a get together with Jesus was chosen to convey an unsavory meeting is anyone's guess, though we do find it interesting that other religions don't have their own version.

For example, a *Come to Vishnu Meeting* just doesn't seem to have the same negative ramifications as one with Jesus. You don't believe you're about to be fired if your boss tells you he needs to see you for a *Come to Vishnu Meeting*, do you? In fact, you might just think it's a good thing.

Namaste.

Replacement phrases: Important meeting; Meeting; Reprimand

See also: *Light a Fire Under*

30,000-Pound Gorilla

"Careful, Bill. You never know what might be coming down the pipe."

Coming Down the Pike (Pipe?)

Before we can anoint this an annoying phrase, we ought to agree on whether it's *coming down the pipe* or *coming down the pike*.

Honestly, we've heard it both ways about an equal number of times. This tells us that half of the annoying folks uttering this are saying it wrong. Doubly annoying.

Officially, every respectable source indicates the correct annoying phrase is *coming down the pike*; and that pike means a large road – think turnpike.

Once we understand this, we're allowed to not only be annoyed at those who say *coming down the pipe*, but we can also make fun of them. They're not just annoying, they're annoying idiots.

However, for our purposes, let's stick with the correct annoying usage of this term. Does anyone you know – and we mean anyone – speak about a road using the word pike? Nope? Same here.

In fact, to everyone we know, a pike is a fish. A big, ugly, mean, freshwater fish. So, whatever is *coming down the pike* sounds like nothing we want to catch.

Managers who want to describe their company's latest and greatest as, "You're going to love what we have *coming down the pike*," need to be shunned. If you're such a manager, please shun yourself.

Instead of using archaic clichés, try describing what's really happening in words the kids will understand. For example, "You're going to love our next product release."

See, wasn't that easy?

Replacement phrases: No replacement needed. Instead of reaching for an outdated cliché, say what you mean, m'kay?

See also: *Incremental Improvement*

30,000-Pound Gorilla

"I'm just having trouble connecting with my peers, that's all."

Connect With

What are we, Legos?

Why is it so many in our midst are always trying to *connect with* so many others?

If you're selling a B2B product or service, you're often told in order to be successful you need to *connect with* as many important people as possible. You're told to *connect with* the decision maker; to *connect with* the department head; to *connect with* the buyer; to *connect with* their coworkers.

Enough with the connecting! Instead, why don't we just meet each other? Why don't we just interact like humans instead of connecting like ubiquitous plastic blocks?

Of course, the biggest annoyance factor for this term comes in its overuse by some managers. You know the type, they start every sentence with *so* and they're constantly discussing, deliberating, contemplating, and bragging about the number of people with whom they're connecting.

Funny thing, of course, is these are most often the same people others try to avoid. Other will connect begrudgingly because the annoyer will hound them forever if they do not. Moreover, their connections, because the annoyer is so focused on quantity instead of quality, are always the shallowest.

Certainly, you know the type. Those whose LinkedIn profiles boast their number of connections – as if connections were dollars. Ugh.

Real relationships – especially in business – are not the prize of some contest; they are the result of genuine human interactions that develop over time. What's more, the person with the most connections doesn't win anything other than a prize for being the most annoying person you know.

Replacement phrases: Meet; Speak to; Interact with

See also: *Face Time; Touch Base*

30,000-Pound Gorilla

"Well, it turns out she was right. She could care less."

Could Care Less

To be clear, the more popular (and correct) version of this one – couldn't care less – would've made the cut of annoying phrases if not for the off-the-charts annoyance factor of *could care less*.

When your annoying manager smugly tells you, "I *could care less*," is he or she saying they actually care a little? Are they saying they care a lot? Are they saying they care more about this than anything in the entire world?

Because, of course, that's what we hear.

As annoying as the egotistical "couldn't care less" sounds, at least it's correct. When you say you couldn't care less, at least you're telling the rest of us exactly how you feel. You don't care about whatever it is we're discussing. In fact, it would not be possible for you or any human to care less about this, right?

We get it. You're a jerk… but we get the gist.

Telling the team you *could care less* tells us you're not just an ass, you're a dumbass; and you make us question why we ever came to work here in the first place. Of course, if we quit, you'd just tell everyone you *could care less*.

Replacement phrases: I'm not interested; That's not important

See also: *Out of Pocket*

30,000-Pound Gorilla

"You were right. It was a bad idea to put the crawlers ahead of the walkers and runners."

Crawl, Walk, Run

Oh, thank you, you kings and queens of caution. Where would we be if you didn't constantly warn us about every new procedure, project, or plan? Your words of wisdom – explaining that we should *crawl, walk, run* – keep us from running immediately, walking before we crawl, or continuing to crawl throughout.

You believe your words keep us focused, and you're right. They keep us focused on the fact that you're an annoying nanny; one who believes we are all just a bunch of hyperactive children who might break a leg or pull a muscle or stub a toe.

Crawl, walk, run is annoying on the surface, as it implies we're all too dumb to figure out how to proceed on our own. Moreover, it's annoying in its overuse.

Those who lecture others to *crawl, walk, run* find ways to shoehorn this maddening phrase into every directive – while somehow also finding a way to sound more condescending with each utterance.

If only there was a *crawl, walk, run* setting on your mouth – we'd set it to newborn.

Replacement phrases: No replacement needed; we're not children.

See also: *Go Slow to Go Fast*

30,000-Pound Gorilla

"We had to fire the first attorney handling the case. It seems he kept dotting the t's and crossing the i's."

Cross the T's and Dot the I's

First, if you ever hear someone explaining how they need to *cross the t's and dot the i's*, you should snicker on the inside, as this overused, annoying saying was originally "dot the i's and cross the t's."

No less annoying when uttered correctly, just interesting so many people screw it up. The origin of this saying is in doubt, though we subscribe to the school of thought that this originated in school.

That is, it was advice provided by teachers of grammar school students to be certain the kids remembered to dot their i's and cross their t's when writing in cursive. (For the Millennials and Gen Zs enjoying this tome, cursive writing is something we did in the olden days.)

Of course, when writing in cursive, the i's and t's are written without their respective dots and crosses until the writer reaches the end of a word. The writer must then pick up his or her pen or pencil from the paper and go back to dot their i's and/or cross their t's. Without doing so, the reader wouldn't know if a vertical line in a word was supposed to be an i, an l, a t, or something else.

Enough history.

Since cursive is no longer taught in America's schools – and since those who overuse this phrase are no longer in school – let's agree to stop saying it altogether. With virtually every document of any importance having been created on a computer for more than three decades, there is no need to remind anyone to *cross the t's and dot the i's* ever again. Doing so just makes you sound silly.

Replacement phrases: Complete the paperwork; Verify everything; Ensure the details are correct; Be precise

See also: *How the Sausage is Made*

30,000-Pound Gorilla

"Imagine how much work Gary could get done if he wasn't so focused on crushing it?"

Crushing It

Yes, this is the title of a best-selling book. Of course, that doesn't mean it's not annoying or misused by your managers and peers. (And yes, it's actually a bit annoying as a book title, but then Steve titled his first book *Sh*t Sandwich*, so who are we to judge?)

Uttered by the ultrapreneurs (entrepreneurs who are really, really, really entrepreneurs) in your life, *crushing it* signifies more than merely reaching your goals or even winning. *Crushing it* is the embodiment of totally dominating every ion opposed to your success and overcoming the greatest adversity one human being has ever endured.

Those who are *crushing it* liken their struggle to that of Viktor Frankl or a Marine charging a heavily-fortified enemy artillery position with only his M16. Their seemingly never-ending journey — as they crush every potential speed bump on their road to success — is more important than the goal.

In fact, they prove this by keeping the rest of us abreast of everything they crush along the way. They tell us how they wake up fighting as they "rise and grind" every morning. God forbid they're slow to rise or need an extra long shower to get moving — that would be, well, not *crushing it*.

Those who are *crushing it* employ social media and blogs to chronicle their battle against their powerful archenemies; fighting such mighty foes as mediocrity, average, leisure, and the dreaded satisfaction. Those who are truly *crushing it* will tell you with delight that they are never satisfied. Satisfaction, you see, if for the weak.

Pity them, as we do..

Replacement phrases: No replacement; just stop saying it, and especially stop writing it. The normal humans in your life are laughing at you.

See also: *Grind; Hustle; Next Level*

Andazola began questioning his vocational choices on his very first day of work.

Currently Now

Annoyingly redundant, isn't it?

When we hear arrogant managers use *currently now*, we want to scream. What is the goal here? Are they trying to over emphasize the present? Do they need everyone hyper-focused on what's happening right now... currently... as we speak... at this moment?

If you're a member of the annoying horde using this term, ask yourself, "As opposed to what? Currently, later?"

It's one or the other! Either say now or say currently. Or, to be fair, say neither. Try omitting both from your sentence and see if it's not just as clear as when you feel the need to spew *currently now* from your mouth.

For example, instead of saying, "We feel the situation *currently now* is worse than at any time in the past." Try saying, "We feel the situation is worse than at any time in the past."

Notice how clean that second sentence is? Notice how it means exactly the same thing even though we didn't include *currently now*?

Here's a quick lesson for the grammar-challenged among you: "is" is a verb that already indicates the present tense. You know, *currently now*?

Replacement phrases: Now; Currently. Or, simply omit both and see if your message is clearer.

See also: *Net-Net; Go Forward Basis*

30,000-Pound Gorilla

"I'm sorry to be the one to tell you this, but you've been cut from the team."

Cut the Mustard

The real question should not be why someone cannot *cut the mustard* at your work; it should be who can?

Really, how is this even possible? Every time we try to *cut the mustard*, the two sides just blob back together. Yes, we can *cut the mustard*, but we cannot keep it cut.

Again, who can?

Another old saying with an unclear origin, managers who use *cut the mustard* to indicate someone's worth to the team or to a project have simply run out of ways to say things. They're grabbing outdated clichés because they either cannot find the proper words to use or they're just lazy.

Overuse of clichés is a sure sign of lazy language. Clichés, you see, are easy. Finding and using the right words takes a little bit of thinking.

Saying you're not sure whether someone can *cut the mustard* could have numerous meanings. Do you think they're incapable? Do you think they're capable, just not willing? Do you think they're capable and willing, though without the assistance required?

What the hell do you mean?

Okay… then just say that and save the mustard cutting for a fun challenge at the next kids' party you host.

Replacement phrases: Able; Capable; Effective

See also: *Pass Muster*

30,000-Pound Gorilla

"I think we'll name him 'Brad's Promotion'. What do you think, Brad?"

Dead in the Water

If we can't agree on every annoying phrase in this book, can we at least agree the morbid slang used in business needs to go?

Dead in the water, like all other dark corporate jargon, is grossly misused. While the speaker intends to convey the message that a project, deal, proposal, relationship, or employee has been or will be canceled, ended, or terminated, relaying to us that something is *dead in the water* is, well, overkill.

Moreover, like that sentence, it's annoying overkill.

If you take a moment to think about it, saying someone is *dead in the water* is pretty gross. They're bloated and discolored and putrid. Yuck.

Sure, for the purists reading this, *dead in the water* is a reference to an immobile boat; therefore, its use means merely that something is stalled. No matter; enough of the rest of humanity believes this refers to a dead body that it goes beyond simply irritating.

We have a novel idea: why don't we think before we speak? Furthermore, instead of defaulting to clichés, let's say exactly what we mean… in plain language… using no metaphors… with the fewest syllables possible.

Try this: "The project is on hold."

See, wasn't that clear, concise, and whole lot less disgusting than telling us, "The project is *dead in the water?*"

Replacement phrases: Canceled; Ended; Terminated; Done; Stalled

See also: *Beat a Dead Horse*

30,000-Pound Gorilla

"We hired Jenny from Domino's Pizza. She's the only one who always completes her deliverables in under 30 minutes."

Deliverables

Pizzas are *deliverables*. Books are *deliverables*. Shoes are *deliverables*.

Everything else? Well, if it has to do with deadlines, tasks, goals, promises, or action plans in your business; then these are deadlines, tasks, goals, promises, or action plans.

Describing your duties as *deliverables* is an attempt to make you sound smarter and the task more important. Unfortunately for you, you do not sound smarter when employing annoying jargon.

Like most of the annoying terms in this book, uttering (or, especially, over-uttering) *deliverables* makes you sound like a disconnected prima donna… of average intelligence.

Truly smart people say what they mean, and they mean what they say. If they need their team to complete certain tasks by a given deadline, they'll communicate this clearly.

Instead of leaning on words and phrases you heard a twenty-something CEO say on CNBC, try speaking in clear terms that ensures everyone knows exactly what it is they can expect from you, and what you expect from them.

Then, sit back and watch them really deliver those *deliverables*!

Replacement phrases: Promises; Tasks

See also: *Action Item*

"Because Oglesby suffers from Satanophobia, he avoids the details."

Devil is in the Detail

This idiom has a simple meaning: A task or project that appears simple on the surface usually has unknown difficulties.

Used correctly, this one is mildly annoying. However, when your manager utters it, it becomes especially irritating. The most prevalent use (and overuse) of *devil is in the detail* – where it's morphed to only mean nefarious intentions – makes us cringe.

Of course, its cringe-worthiness turns exponential when your manager shoehorns *devil is in the detail* anywhere he or she likes. Once an annoying manager hears *devil is in the detail* spoken for the first time, he or she latches onto it and suddenly the *devil is in the detail*… every detail… of every project, task, or contract.

No longer is anything as it seems because, of course, the *devil is in the detail*.

Your manager uses this one so often you're not even sure what it means – you just know it's coming out of his/her mouth at least once per meeting.

Given this, we suppose your manager could be partially correct – certainly, every meeting starts to feels like you're in hell.

Replacement phrases: No replacement needed; just stop saying it.

See also: *It's All in the Details; Lost in the Sauce*

30,000-Pound Gorilla

"I told you we needed someone to direct the traffic on this one."

Direct the Traffic

Apparently, your office has become so crowded and hectic your annoying manager needs you to *direct the traffic*. Without someone completing this important duty, everyone would surely crash into each other. It would create chaos… mass hysteria.

It seems for every project – whether important or not – many annoying bosses will assign someone to *direct the traffic*. You'll hear matter-of-factly, "I'll need you to *direct the traffic* on this one."

You'll twitch, cringe, and perhaps even want to lay on the floor in the fetal position.

Not, of course, because of this one irritating phrase, but because it never stops. It never changes. Your annoying boss cannot help himself or herself.

Your manager belongs to a massive, secret, cult-like organization created to make employees' ears bleed. This group simply cannot speak without inserting an idiom, metaphor, analogy, or other equally-aggravating phrase – even when (or especially when) the correct term is shorter or even more descriptive.

They cannot be stopped.

Just do your best to *direct the traffic*, collect your check, go home, cry a little, and drink a lot.

Replacement phrases: Direct; Take charge

See also: *Run Interference*

30,000-Pound Gorilla

The company didn't know what they were getting when they hired Conner; a self-described true disruptor.

Disruptor

Almost no one labeled a *disruptor* is really disrupting much of anything. Heck, today's *disruptors* are barely even *change agents*.

Most often, of course, *disruptors* are called *disruptors* because they call themselves *disruptors*.

Just as shortcuts and tips are now annoyingly called *hacks*, for some people, old-fashioned working has become disrupting; managers have become *disruptors*. These days, it's not enough to just help your business grow; you've got to disrupt an entire industry.

Self-described *disruptors* are also the ultrapreneurs who will tell you they're *crushing it* as they go about being nothing more than CEOs of one-person companies trapped in the gig economy.

That is, they pick up the crumbs left by true *disruptors*, tell the world how hard they're *hustling 24/7/365*, and proceed to change nothing before they move on to their next disruptive idea (that also never seems to pan out).

If you're old enough to remember the world before social media, self-described *disruptors* are just like the guy at work who always told everyone how hard he was working. Of course, he was the one accomplishing the least.

True *disruptors* don't call themselves *disruptors*, they just disrupt. If you fancy yourself a *disruptor* and use that word out loud, everyone you work with thinks you're an annoying, pompous prick.

Instead of telling us how much you're disrupting, just start disrupting… we'll notice.

Replacement phrases: No replacement phrase needed; just stop saying it.

See also: *Change Agent; Thought Leader; Game Changer*

30,000-Pound Gorilla

"Barbara has always been our deep dive specialist when it comes to vetting suppliers."

Do a Deep Dive

Embarrassingly, we've caught ourselves saying this all too often. Sometimes, we just can't help it… it just comes out of our mouths before we have a chance to catch ourselves. If it makes you feel any better, we sternly admonish ourselves in our heads when *do a deep dive* finds its way out.

Unless you're wearing SCUBA gear, or you're eleven years old and your annoying uncle just threw a quarter into the deep end of the pool, you're likely not going to *do a deep dive* on anything.

You're going to analyze or inspect something. Heck, sometimes you're just promising simply to read something when you announce your plans to *do a deep dive*.

Providing additional color in your language is not necessarily a bad thing for managers; but, overusing this color or allowing the color to get in the way of a simple message is lazy… and annoying.

Instead of telling someone to *do a deep dive* into a topic to see what they find, simply ask them to analyze it. It means the same thing, but your message is clearer (and you're much less annoying) using the latter.

You're welcome.

Replacement phrases: Analyze; Inspect; Read

See also: *Drill Down; Teat Down, The*

30,000-Pound Gorilla

"Okay, I want a clean fight. No leg humping and no sniffing below the belt."

Dog in this Fight

From the Southern United States comes this annoying idiom that means nothing more than whether you care about the outcome of some event.

"I don't have a *dog in this fight*," means you don't care. Conversely, "I have a *dog in this fight*," means you do.

So, you ask, why not just say that?

Because that would be too easy. Instead, we suppose managers want to sound hip or cool by regurgitating some old southern slang. Of course, telling someone about your *dog in this fight* just makes you sound like a Redneck – certainly not what you were hoping for.

Moreover, *dog in this fight* is a reference to illegal dog fighting. You know, that back-alley activity supported by those with no conscience or morals that will get you booted off an NFL team and sent to federal prison for 21 months?

To make this annoying phrase even worse (or better, depending on how you look at it), many managers will misuse the term and tell you they don't have a "dog in this hunt" or a "dog in this race."

We guess these are better, since they don't conjure up images of dead canine companions.

Though, to be clear, misquoting a hackneyed cliché makes you sound more than just annoying. It makes you sound annoyingly uneducated.

Replacement phrases: Interest; Vested Interest

See also: *Skin in the Game*

30,000-Pound Gorilla

"Hiring smart employees was a double-edged sword for you. On the one hand, they helped your department reach its goals. On the other, we no longer need you."

Double-Edged Sword

Seriously, aren't at least half of all swords double-edged? We'll venture to guess that more than 75% of swords are doubled-edged.

So, why then is a *double-edged sword* treated as something unique? Moreover, why does it mean something with both favorable and unfavorable consequences?

A *double-edged sword* does not mean a sword with two blades instead of a blade and a handle; it simply implies the sword has the same sharp edge on both sides of the blade.

Someone using a *double-edged sword* would know this, right? Shouldn't we assume they would employ both edges to their advantage in a sword fight? Yet, we warn them something is a *double-edged sword*. That doesn't make any sense.

But you may ask, why is it annoying?

There are two reasons this term deserves its place in this book. First, its overuse. Annoying managers who grab hold of annoying phrases are like pit bulls — they never let go. Those who like to use *double-edged sword* cannot stop using it. Everything becomes a *double-edged sword* in their world.

"Drinking coffee after eleven is a *double-edged sword*."

"Scoring a great parking space in front of the office is a *double-edged sword*."

"Finding lint in your belly button is a *double-edged sword*."

Yes, it can and does border on the absurd!

The second reason *double-edged sword* made the cut of annoying business phrases is that even when used correctly, it's employed more as a warning of the potential bad outcomes by managers afraid to make decisions.

"That's a real *double-edged sword*; are we sure it makes sense for us to proceed?" These managers are weak, skittish;, and more concerned about their bonuses than driving the business forward.

Cowards! All of them! And, I think we can all agree the only thing more annoying that a cliché-spewing, pompous turd-of-a-manager is a weak, indecisive turd-of-a-manager.

Replacement phrases: No replacement needed; just mention the potential pitfalls of a decision, if any.

See also: *Analysis Paralysis*

30,000-Pound Gorilla

"This new system is great. It allows us to download new information to everyone all at once."

Download

Used properly, *download* has a place in the business world.

If only this were the case in virtually every office in America – yours included. Unfortunately for you, *download* has come to mean everything from being updated on a major project to simply reading a memo.

Steve once attended a meeting where the manager used *download* to mean five different activities by his team. He wanted one employee to *download* all the information he had on a particular customer; another to get a *download* from the service department on an issue; another to ask for a *download* from the phone vendor on how to use a new feature; another to *download* everything we knew about a new program from the manufacturer; and still another to be sure and give anyone not in attendance a complete *download* of the meeting.

Annoying? Excruciatingly.

In each of these instances, the manager simply meant for someone to gather information.

Some pompous managers are also using *download* to describe one's ability or capacity to comprehend complicated information or to complete certain tasks.

We've heard, "He doesn't have the *download* speed for something like this."

Of course, none of these misuses of *download* can match the idiocy or annoyance factor of those rare managers who confuse *download* with down low; as in, "Be sure to keep this on the *download*."

WTH?

Sadly, we've heard that cringeworthy sentence more than once in the workplace; and once you hear it, you cannot unhear it… ever.

Replacement phrases: Gather information; Read; Acquire; Disseminate

See also: *Do a Deep Dive; Bandwidth*

30,000-Pound Gorilla

"That's what I like about Paschal; he really tries to drill down on what his employees are thinking."

Drill Down

When clarity is necessary, managers will often ask you to *drill down* on something. The meaning is usually clear: They want more information, and they believe this information is hidden or otherwise beyond the superficial view they've been provided.

Sounds fine, right? Actually, it is. *Drill down*, by itself, is not necessarily an annoying business term. *Drill down* can be a useful direction provided from a supervisor.

However, as with so many terms in this book, *drill down* morphs to have an almost ubiquitous meaning, and becomes something managers clutch onto… and never let go. Suddenly, you find yourself being asked to *drill down* on anything and everything – without a verifiable need for more information.

Drill down becomes a catchall phrase for everything from approving an invoice to simply reading a document. "Let's *drill down* on that report;" "I need you to *drill down* on this account;" "Could you *drill down* on that email?"

When your manager latches onto a phrase, it becomes annoying. But when she warps the original meaning and begins to insert it into nearly every sentence, it makes your ears bleed.

Our only advice to maintain your sanity is to make these phrases into a drinking game. If your manager is overusing an annoying phrase, discuss this with your team and agree everyone will take a drink (of their coffee, their water, from the flask in their jacket) each time your manager uses one of these terms in a meeting.

You're welcome – your meetings will forever become tolerable.

Replacement phrases: Investigate; Inspect; Verify; Approve

See also: *Do a Deep Dive; Download*

30,000-Pound Gorilla

Mobley was famous for always making his team drink from a firehose at every meeting.

Drink from a Firehose

This one annoys us for two reasons: First, its overuse; and, of course, its needless exaggeration.

To literally attempt to *drink from a firehose* would, at the very least, rip the skin from your face. More likely, it would decapitate you. Either way, the imagery is disturbing.

Managers love to throw this one around when they're presented with or presenting a vast amount of information in a relatively short time. They believe that attempting to ingest an excess of data is analogous to trying to *drink from a firehose*.

It never is. It's never even been close.

While some presenters are prone to share more information, advice, or opportunities than an individual or team can easily assimilate and put into practice, no one has ever delivered the equivalent of a firehose worth.

This makes *drink from a firehose* an unnecessary exaggeration. If only it stopped there.

Managers, as you know from multiple entries in this book, tend to compile and forever employ sayings they should otherwise discard. This leads them to overuse and even shoehorn these phrases into virtually every situation – making the exaggerations even more egregious.

If you're a manager who feels like every delivery of information you receive is akin to taking a *drink from a firehose*, then perhaps you're just not very smart. Perhaps, as most of your employees probably already know, you're just a little slow on the uptake. Stop confirming this with your annoying sayings.

You sound a lot smarter to the rest of us when your mouth is closed.

Replacement phrases: No replacement needed; just stop saying it.

See also: *Trying to Boil the Ocean*

30,000-Pound Gorilla

"Oh no!"

Drink/Drank the Kool-Aid

There's no doubt the worst thing about uttering this saying is that it originated from the 1978 Jonestown Massacre – an incomprehensible tragedy where over 900 people died in a mass murder-suicide by drinking drug-laced Kool-Aid.

If that's not enough to have you stop saying this annoying phrase, we've got nothing.

Well, maybe not nothing. Even if you don't know the phrase's origins, you surely understand that asking someone to *drink the Kool-Aid* is akin to asking them to commit to a cult-like organization or project, right?

Of course, most managers who repeat this annoying phrase do so in an accusatory way. They claim others (those not as enlightened as themselves) are so easily deluded or manipulated that they *drank the Kool-Aid*.

To prove their own superiority, they'll let you know when they think a rival "really *drank the Kool-Aid*." Translation: He's dumb; I'm smart. He's a sheep; I'm a freethinker.

Certainly, your employees know the truth… at least those who didn't *drink the Kool-Aid* you're serving.

Replacement phrases: Agree; Believe

See also: *Buy-In*

30,000-Pound Gorilla

"When I gave him the drop-dead date, I didn't think he'd take it literally."

Drop-Dead Date

If you've held a real job for more than five minutes, you know most managers like to overemphasize everything. To these managers, facts aren't nearly enough to make their point. Indeed, even facts delivered with emphasis aren't nearly enough to properly and clearly define the urgency of a given matter.

Drop-dead date is a perfect example.

This annoying bit of business jargon simply means deadline. That's the fact here… it's a deadline. If a manager wanted to redundantly emphasize deadline, he or she would use "final deadline."

But no, not your manager. For your manager, neither facts nor facts with emphasis are enough for everyone on the team to understand the importance of completing something by a certain date.

Your manager, that brilliant thinker who uses words like *hustle* and *grind* to prove how dedicated and hardworking he is, tells you a project has a *drop-dead date* and not simply a deadline.

Of course, for the rest of us, hearing *drop-dead date* makes us wish someone would.

Replacement phrases: Deadline

See also: *Ask, The; Deliverables*

30,000-Pound Gorilla

"Playford is one of our best managers; always on the lookout in case his team drops the ball."

Drop the Ball

As demonstrated throughout this book, sports idioms are the most overused annoying things managers say.

When sports terms are a bit obscure and not overused – like hat trick, for example – these sayings can have both meaning and impact. In automotive retail, selling three cars in a single day is often referred to as a hat trick. This is a hockey term (at least as far as those of us in the US are concerned) meaning three goals in a game scored by a single player.

This is an appropriate use of a sports metaphor that doesn't come off as pompous or annoying. It's also not a misuse – while, for example, trifecta would be in these instances. (A trifecta refers to a bet where the bettor correctly picks the first three finishers in a race in order.)

Drop the ball, unfortunately, doesn't share the same novelty (or forgiveness) for using a sports term in business as hat trick.

It's annoying on the surface because it usually indicates someone failed or otherwise made an error. It's also annoying (like most of the phrases in this book) in its overuse. Moreover, it's annoying in its overly-broad meaning.

We've heard *drop the ball* used by the same manager to cover everything from screwing up a major proposal to someone forgetting to make the coffee in the morning. It can't mean both things, right? One is clearly a more egregious blunder than the other, correct?

After all, it's unforgivable to forget to make the coffee.

Replacement phrases: Forget; Fail

See also: *Shit the Bed; Screw the Pooch*

As a former dominatrix, Kelly never had an issue keeping her ducks in a row.

Ducks in a Row

There are multiple theories you can find online attempting to ascertain the origin of *ducks in a row* – some even arguing it's from the 1700s. Frankly, we don't care where the term originated, just that it exits the lexicon of today's businesspeople.

Coincidentally, the annoying managers who use this fowl phrase are often the Mother Hen types. That is, they're those overprotective, caring nurturers whose teams never seem to accomplish much above mediocrity.

Not that it's a bad thing to care about your team, it isn't; but the Mother Hens in the business world never seem to let their flock stray too far from the nest. Consequently, their subordinates don't take risks, so they don't reap the rewards of the risk-takers.

Mother Hens are best described as the helicopter parents of the business world; and they're the ones who constantly remind their charges to keep their *ducks in a row*. Furthermore, these Mother Hens step in and help their teams keep their *ducks in a row*. Ugh.

To the Mother Hens in business, we can only ask why? Are you afraid one of your baby ducks is going to be savagely eaten by stray fox? Why not drop the Mother Hen act and start leading?

As the old proverb goes, "Put a man's *ducks in a row* and you'll feed him for a day; Hold a man accountable to keeping his own *ducks in a row* and you'll feed him for a lifetime."

Or something like that.

Replacement phrases: Orderly; In order; Put first things first

See also: *Herding Cats*

30,000-Pound Gorilla

Everything is... isn't it?

Easier Said that Done

When your annoying manager tells you something is *easier said than done*, you have our permission to reply, "No shit, Sherlock. Everything, and I mean everything, is *easier said than done.*"

Seriously, name one thing that's easier to do than to say? Oh, and don't get philosophical on us and reply, "Loving someone is often easier to do than to say." Do you want us to vomit?

Everything is *easier said than done*. Ehv Ree Thing. Everything.

If something is difficult, then say difficult. If something is virtually impossible, say virtually impossible. When a manager tells you something is *easier said than done*, they're telling you they're an idiot. They're telling you they don't understand basic physics or even math.

This phrase is annoying because it's nonsensical; it's annoying on its idiocy. Stop saying it and you'll immediately sound smarter.

Of course, as you probably already know, that's *easier said than done*.

Replacement phrases: Difficult; Impossible

See also: *Are Two Different Things; It Is What It Is*

30,000-Pound Gorilla

Fred always had trouble eating his own dog food.

Eat Your Own Dog Food

Like more than a few of the annoying phrases in this book, *eat your own dog food* conjures up unpleasant imagery. Of course, like every annoying thing managers utter, unpleasant imagery won't stop them from spewing tired, exasperating, hackneyed phrases at every turn.

This term originated as a way to describe companies that use (or at least test) their own products within their ranks before (and after) releasing these to the public. If that were its only use, we suppose it wouldn't make the list of the most annoying things managers say.

Unfortunately, it's not.

Today, *eat your own dog food* is most often misused as a nauseating way to say, "those in glass houses shouldn't throw stones." In other words, don't talk about our problems until you address your own problems.

While we don't hear this one too often, Steve was lucky enough to hear a service manager at a car dealership yell this at the store's sales manager while he was writing this book. The sales manager was complaining that the service department's mistakes were hurting the store's sales business. This prompted the service manager to yell, "Don't fucking come in here with that shit until you guys learn to *eat your own dog food*."

Colorful? Yes, colorful and confusing; as the sales manager just walked away shaking his head, while the service manager immediately sported a shit-eating grin and a look of "mission accomplished" on his face.

As you could predict, ultimately nothing changed, and both managers continued to think the other was the real problem.

Replacement phrases: No replacement needed; just say what you mean.

See also: *Shit Where You Eat*

30,000-Pound Gorilla

"I guess it's time we talked about the elephant in the room. His name is Doug, and he's lousy at hide and seek."

Elephant in the Room

This phrase is annoying in its stupidity. There, we said it.

The *elephant in the room* refers to that (almost always negative) thing everyone is aware of, but no one wants to address. It's just there, in plain sight, and on the top of everyone's mind… but, no one wants to talk about it.

This is stupid because who the heck wouldn't want to talk about an *elephant in the room*? Holy crap, that would be amazing… and frightening… and probably cramped.

It's the first thing we'd mention if we walked into a room with an elephant present. We'd probably shriek like a schoolgirl and say something inappropriate like, "Holy shit, that's a fucking elephant! How in the fuck did they get that fucking elephant in here?"

If you wanted a more appropriate phrase for business — something everyone was aware of, but no one wanted to address — you should probably change this to "fart in the room." No one wants to talk about a fart; even if everyone smells it.

Because, as you know, he who smelt it dealt it.

Replacement phrases: Problem; Issue; Fart in the room

See also: *800-Pound Gorilla*

30,000-Pound Gorilla

"This is unfortunate; I was really hoping to get some face time with you today."

Face Time

Someone wanting to meet with you… strike that. A self-important douche wanting to meet with you face-to-face will often ask for some *face time*. As in, "We've definitely got to get some *face time* during this conference."

This douchey manager thinks *face time* is the hip way the kids say meeting. As with all assumptions made by douches, he's wrong on this one… way wrong.

Hearing that someone wants *face time* with you is especially annoying because it's always delivered by the most insincere people you know. They're sycophants, so they're naturally insincere in all their relationships. In fact, their insincerity is so severe, they don't even hear themselves.

Insincere sycophants (redundant, we know) believe their words and sticky-sweet tone are enough to convince you they're good people (because they think your IQ is well below theirs). They're not good people.

They want *face time*, for crap's sake. Truly good people don't want *face time*; truly good people want to meet; they want to talk; they want to *connect with* you… strike that. Truly good people just want to catch up.

Replacement phrases: Meeting; Discussion

See also: *Connect With*

30,000-Pound Gorilla

As head of IT, Tilley was determined his cubicle would be properly firewalled from the others.

Firewalled

A (sometimes) business partner of Steve's was too busy to join him on a new project; and told him he was "*firewalled* for the foreseeable future" and couldn't help. Of course, it took Steve a few seconds to decipher what he meant; and once Steve did, he was (and still is) embarrassed for him.

What in the hell is a grown person – especially an executive – doing trying to replace a simple adjective like busy with a bastardized version of a noun?

This, of course, goes to the very heart of the self-important in the business world – the very reason this book was written.

Many in the business world believe they are somehow cooler, hipper, more important when their verbosity takes an idiotic turn like this. They are, of course, not. They are just the opposite.

To be clear, *firewalled* is not really a proper word; it's slang. *Firewalled* is sort of a past participle of firewall (if firewall was a verb… it's not).

A firewall, for the uninformed, is a barrier that prevents the spread of a fire from one part of a structure (like a ship or a building) to another. For example, there is a firewall in your car that separates the engine compartment from you.

In the world of computing, a firewall is the technology that keeps the computers in your office (relatively) safe from the outside world of malware and viruses.

Knowing this, when Steve's colleague told him that he was *firewalled*, Steve should've assumed he was being protected from the outside, harmful world. More like a cocoon, we suppose. Of course, if that was the case, Steve wouldn't really want his help on the new project, would he?

Replacement phrases: Busy; Unavailable

See also: *Hard Stop*

30,000-Pound Gorilla

Sadly, the company never had a chance to sell the client after the team misunderstood the full-court press strategy.

Full-Court Press

You really want to – we mean really, really want to – impress the client, and we get it. But, do you have to explain this to us using multiple crappy sports metaphors?

"Alright, it's *game time* folks, I really need everyone to *play ball* and put the *full-court press* on this client. Scoring this account will be a *game changer*, we simply can't afford to *drop the ball* this time."

Ugh. Kill us now.

A *full-court press* in business is akin to pulling out all the stops, going all the way, or throwing everything you have at the goal. Given that *full-court press* is a defensive strategy meant to pressure and slow down the offense in basketball, how does this translate into pulling out all the stops in business?

It doesn't.

Nearly always, by the way, the *full-court press* is meant to impress the subject of your efforts – it's almost never used to merely discuss how you're going to attack a goal. Regardless of the business usage, how does any of this equate to playing tough defense?

It doesn't.

Full-court press is just another in a long list of annoying sports idioms that sound tough or committed but should never have been included in the lexicon of the business world.

Unfortunately, like nearly everyone reading this, we're stuck with the rah-rah crowd of annoying managers (the most annoying of all) who grab any sports saying they can find and beat it to death.

Our death.

Replacement phrases: Impress; Do your best

See also: *Give 110%*

"FYI, it looks like the MTD ROI is so low you're going to want to CYA."

FYI

To be clear, reading the abbreviation *FYI* in an email or text from your boss is perfectly acceptable. It makes sense, given the brevity that typed text often demands. *FYI*, after all, means for your information… and that's a lot to type if you spelled it out.

However, hearing *FYI* from these same folks (especially in a meeting), and our douche-meter goes above eleven.

FYI is almost unforgivable as it's often used as a pompous way to put others down. For example, "*FYI*, I was club champion for three years running."

When someone inserts *FYI* in their comment to you, they're most often trying to exercise some superiority over you. Don't believe me? Listen for the next five *FYI*s you hear directed at you. We guarantee more than four of these are meant to put you and your little brain in place.

The bad news in business is that you cannot stop pomposity. Therefore, what can you do to combat those who overuse *FYI*?

The answer for us is to turn *FYI* around on the pretentious hordes and give it a new meaning. An exercise that we love (believe us, it's very cathartic) is to use *FYI* as a polite way to say, "fuck you, idiot." You see, that's F (fuck) Y (you) I (idiot).

For example, when some arrogant manager is telling you black is white and white is black – and they include a pompous *FYI* in their diatribe – we like to retort with, "Well, *FYI* …." Telling this manager, "fuck you, idiot…" in our minds.

This is sometimes very liberating. Though, at the very least, it always makes us smile.

Life – especially at work – is about the little victories, after all.

Replacement phrases: Often, there is no replacement needed. *FYI* is just an extra, unneeded abbreviation.

See also: *ASAP*

30,000-Pound Gorilla

Coach Larson's career may have been short, but he was nothing if not a game changer.

Game Changer

By the way, it's not just *game changer*, it's also game changing, and any other iteration of change combined with game that makes for an ear-bleedingly annoying business term.

To be clear, "game anything" is annoying unless you're speaking about an actual game. In business, those prone to exaggeration love to dub everything as a *game changer*.

Honestly, though, how many games have ever really been changed? In the history of all games, sports, and similar activities, how often has one been truly changed; genuinely transformed? The dunk in basketball, the forward pass in football, the designated hitter in baseball. Those were *game changers*.

Today, wearing a shirt designed specifically to be worn untucked has been labeled a *game changer*. Hint: it's not; it's not even an improvement. (Moreover, those of you overpaying for this privilege have been duped.)

In fact, almost nothing crowned as a *game changer* today does anything to change any game, or business, or style, or… you get it.

Labelling every improvement as a *game changer* is the worst kind of faux bluster, and annoying to those of us just trying to keep score.

Replacement phrases: Innovation; Change; Improvement

See also: *Disruptor*

30,000-Pound Gorilla

Spendley never got promoted because he never could devise a good game plan.

Game Plan

You've already been introduced to *game changer* and *bring your 'A' game*, but there are actually four annoying business phrases that include the word game – and that's after rejecting staples like "game ball" and "stay ahead of the game." We could've had a hot half-dozen, but those two idioms don't seem to have the same annoying overuse as the ones that made the cut.

Of those that did make it into print, *game plan* has become the go-to staple for lazy managers incapable of simply describing what they need in one word.

Instead of having a plan, they must have a *game plan*. It's impossible for these annoying souls to simply have an approach; no, they must have a *game plan*. They can't just work on a strategy; they have to *game plan*.

Why? We don't freaking know!

It seems unnecessary and excessive to add in the extra word; though we suppose it makes annoying (or, perhaps, impotent) managers sound more macho when they change a ho-hum word (like plan) into a sports term.

Uttering *game plan* in business has no more importance than any number of simpler, single words.

This begs the question: Why so verbose? Are you overcompensating for something?

That would be our guess.

Replacement phrases: Strategy; Plan

See also: *Game Time*

30,000-Pound Gorilla

"Dawson, I know I said it was game time, but I think you're taking things too literally."

Game Time

Your manager wants to be sure everyone knows today is an important day. Perhaps you're meeting with a new client or the big boss is coming in from corporate. Whatever the event, he announces that it's *game time*.

Game time, of course, doesn't mean we pull out the Scrabble board or grab a deck of cards. It means everyone needs to be ready for action; ready to be on our best behavior; ready to *give 110%*.

Ugh.

Often, those who use this term in the workplace will also clap their hands a few times to emphasize that it truly is *game time*, people!

These annoying managers are also prone to high five employees throughout the day like it's 1985. They'll throw up their hand for a high five or thrust their arm forward for a fist bump for anything they see as an accomplishment.

From landing a new account to simply filling the coffee pot, their subordinates and coworkers are subjected to constant hand slapping followed by the occasional "alright!"

If your manager announces *game time* and only follows this with an awkward high five or a fist bump, you should feel lucky. If this was still 1985, they'd follow that high five with a soft butt slap.

Thankfully, butt slaps are no longer acceptable in the workplace – he knows he'd be fired – otherwise, your butt would feel the love from his hand multiple times a week.

Unfortunately, high fives, fist bumps, and announcements of *game time* won't get him fired.

If only.

Replacement phrases: No replacement needed because it's never really *game time* when you're at work.

See also: *Game Plan*

30,000-Pound Gorilla

"Okay, Burton; as I promised, we got into bed with you. Now will you sign the agreement?"

Get into Bed

Your manager is a misogynist ass, we get it. Now, he's advocating you *get into bed* with a client.

Oh! The! Humanity!

Lighten up, Francis; he's using an idiotic and outdated figure of speech so crude it will likely land him in the human resources office at some point – just not today. Today, he's simply asking you in a completely tired, clichéd way to develop a close business relationship with the client.

He's not asking you to sleep with them – though he's probably wishing you would.

Hearing *get into bed* in today's workplace should make you feel embarrassed for the person saying it. It's outdated; and in an era where a first grader can get suspended for chewing their PB&J sandwich into the shape of a gun, managers should be more careful with their words.

It seems everyone is looking for a reason to be offended or prove their failures-to-date are based on some unseen oppression. If you're an unthinking manager still using *get into bed* instead of "build a relationship," we're hopeful you're very near retirement. If not, your vocabulary needs a 21st Century upgrade.

Replacement phrases: Build a relationship

See also: *Connect With; Face Time*

30,000-Pound Gorilla

"When Brodsky says he gives 110%, he means he gives 30% on Mondays, 30% on Tuesdays, 30% on Wednesdays, 20% on Thursdays, & nothing on Fridays."

Give 110%

We used to cringe when coworkers and managers uttered this useless phrase. Now, we smile because we think, "You lazy bastards! Why stop at 110%? Why not give 111% or 127% or 1,000,000%?"

If 110% is achievable, then even more is possible, right?

This makes us wonder if those advocating for 110% are just bad at math. Do they genuinely believe because of their words someone who was planning to give everything they had will now dig even deeper and find an additional 10% they never knew they possessed?

Give 110% might very well be the genesis of the entire fake motivation movement. Is it possible that if some numbnuts hadn't come up with *give 110%* during the last century, we'd never have to hear how someone is hustling and grinding today?

This phrase is annoying and it's dumb. It's never possible to give 110% to something – 110% is exactly 10% more than everything you've got to give. Once you've given something 100% of your efforts, time, knowledge… whatever; there is no more to give – you've given your all.

Instead of becoming annoyed by those asking you to *give 110%*, feel sorry for them. They're fauxtivationalists who are bad at math. A pitiful combination.

Replacement phrases: Do your best

See also: *Bring Your 'A' Game; Work Smarter, Not Harder; Next Level; Push the Envelope*

30,000-Pound Gorilla

"If my command of the native language is correct, I believe he just promised to give me a heads up."

Give You a Heads Up

Sometimes phrases are annoying just because. *Give you a heads up* is one of these.

We can't quite put our finger on it, but when someone promises to let us know something in advance, we should be thrilled, right? The problem is they verbalize this by saying, "I'm going to be sure to *give you a heads up.*"

Well… thank you, we suppose. Does not telling us mean they're going to give us a heads down?

We understand this means they're going to keep us aware – as in, when you have your head up, you're more aware of your surroundings. Though just because we understand a dumb, overused business phrase doesn't mean we can't be annoyed by it.

And… annoyed we are.

This one is irritating because it's become so widely overused to the point it may never go away. Your grandchildren's grandchildren will likely make multiple, daily promises to "*Give you a heads up.*"

Thank goodness you won't be around to hear that.

Replacement phrases: Give notice

See also: *Headhunter*

30,000-Pound Gorilla

"I quit; but just to be sure you understand what I'm saying, I'll be firewalled and unable to connect with our solutions providers or deliver client engagement on a go forward basis."

Go Forward Basis

Not only is *go forward basis* annoying, it's confusing.

When we hear it, we can only imagine the speaker meant to say something else and *go forward basis* just fell out of his mouth on its own. Is he okay? Did he not get enough sleep last night? Did he just suffer a mini stroke?

If you've never heard *go forward basis*, consider yourself lucky. Once you do, you cannot unhear it. What's worse is any manager who utters *go forward basis* just once will find a way to use it again and again… forever.

Go forward basis is annoying on many levels, though the basest of which is that it most often simply means the same as "moving forward," "from now on," and "beginning today."

Of course, this begs the question: Why not just say "from now on?"

Because, of course, the egomaniacal manager using *go forward basis* is cooler and hipper than us common folk. Most often he's a he… a Millennial… sporting a ridiculous beard… wearing untucked shirts at work… and drinking a coffee that requires more than two words to order.

He's a hipster dufus running a business, and you're stuck with him on a *go forward basis*. Good luck.

Save your faux outrage if you're female or elderly or beardless or wearing your shirt tucked in or enjoy your coffee black and you like to say *go forward basis*, you're also a hipster dufus.

Congratulations.

Replacement phrases: Future; Moving forward; From now on

See also: *Currently Now*

30,000-Pound Gorilla

"I finally hired a real go-getter."

Go-Getter

Today – you annoying manager you – you talk about the *grind* and how much you *hustle*. If we were sitting in your office a century ago, and you wanted to explain to those of us who don't really care about your alleged strong work ethic, you'd describe yourself as a real *go-getter*.

And, as is true today with the grinders and hustlers, your coworkers would hate you even more than they already did.

As annoying as this phrase was a hundred years ago, this antiquated description of someone who aggressively pursues all opportunities has unfortunately never died. While no one today would call themselves a *go-getter*, there are still annoying managers hanging onto this term.

Ask them about that new employee and they'll tell you "he's a real *go-getter*."

Really? Where does he go and what exactly does he get? Also, why is he a "real" *go-getter*? Are there fake *go-getters* out there?

Hmm, now that we write that, we suppose there are. They're the ones posting memes about how hard they're working; how much they *grind*; how much they *hustle*; how they're always *crushing it*.

This makes us genuinely miss the days when we had real *go-getters* among us.

Replacement phrases: Motivated; Aggressive; Hardworking

See also: *Hustle; Grind*

30,000-Pound Gorilla

"I thought the best way for the team to follow your 'go slow to go fast' strategy was swap out their Macs with these Commodore 64s."

Go Slow to Go Fast

This saying made the list of annoying phrases not because it's incorrect or even bad advice – often it's great advice.

No, *go slow to go fast* is included because most every manager using it today doesn't believe it and/or doesn't practice it himself/herself. *Go slow to go fast* is a seemingly contradictory axiom; though similarly to "less is more," when the saying is understood and followed, this advice can help your business reach its goals.

To be clear, *go slow to go fast* is not analogous to *The Tortoise and the Hare*. That fable refers to the value of determination and dedication over speed and shenanigans. *Go slow to go fast* can more correctly be compared to "look before you leap."

However, its original and more precise meaning would be to ensure you have a clear strategy, a decent plan, a goal, and – in the case of a product or service launch – an addressable market before attacking something new.

In other words, proceeding cautiously is prudent and will help you achieve your goals faster than simply throwing a bunch of crap against the walls to see what sticks. Proceeding cautiously is not the same as *analysis paralysis* – you can and should make fast decisions, just be certain they're based on data and support the overriding strategy.

Wait, this isn't supposed to be a lesson on what the saying means or even how to apply it in your business, is it?

Our apologies, we digressed.

This was supposed to be an attack on those managers who drop *go slow to go fast* into virtually every strategy meeting. They do this, of course, because they think it makes them sound smart, sensible and thoughtful.

It does not. It makes them sound like the smug egomaniacs they are.

There, satisfied?

Replacement phrases: Plan; Have a strategy; Make your business case

See also: *Analysis Paralysis*

30,000-Pound Gorilla

"Unfortunately, it does not."

Goes Without Saying

When we hear the mind-numbing phrase *goes without saying*, our immediate thoughts are, "Does it? Does it go without saying? If it does, then why did you say it? You've successfully wasted however many seconds of our lives it took for you to say that thing that *goes without saying*. Congratulations, you are not only annoying, you are a fool. Have a nice day."

We understand the annoying managers in your life very often feel the need to simply fill the air with their vast knowledge and experience. They cannot sit quietly and listen; they cannot let others have the last word; they cannot let others be viewed as the most knowledgeable on any topic.

They must open their traps and regurgitate something we all already clearly understand. Of course, to keep from looking like the sad buffoons they are, they begin their diatribe with, "It *goes without saying*, but…"

The only possible way to eradicate this unnecessary verbal assault on our ears is for us to band together and agree we will all use the same retort. That is, whenever we hear someone start his/her sentence with, "It *goes without saying*," we need to be ready to reply in unison, "Then don't," before they even have a chance to tell us what's so redundantly important to them.

Replacement phrases: Obviously, it *goes without saying* that no replacement is needed.

See also: *Easier Said Than Done; Let Me Start By Saying*

30,000-Pound Gorilla

"I discovered I'm only good with a hammer, so I decided to only hire nails."

Good with a Hammer (So... Everything is a Nail)

Let's not mince words.

He's *good with a hammer so he thinks everything is a nail* is an insult. An insult, like most blatant insults, that is never uttered directly to the person being insulted. This one is delivered by arrogant managers and know-it-all employees behind someone's back.

Managers most often use it to describe a highly-competent direct report or peer who they feel is a likely threat to their leadership. While they begrudgingly recognize the insultee's most pronounced strength (good with a hammer), they claim this is actually a hindrance given the insultee's tunnel vision or lack of awareness (so he thinks everything is a nail).

When used by an employee to describe a boss, they're generally not referring to a strength but rather the singular focus/tactic/strategy how the boss believes he or she will get results. It's an insult of the highest order… and it's annoying in its own lack of awareness.

While we've both worked with more than a few managers who lacked some vision, we've worked with darn few who were so focused on one way of doing things as to believe it was the only way.

If you believe someone is really just *good with a hammer so he thinks everything is a nail*, perhaps you should open your own mind just a tad. Maybe, just maybe, this one is a nail. Or, more likely, perchance the insultee in this case has a few more talents you'll discover if you just try.

Regardless of why you're accusing someone of thinking everything is a nail, the most annoying aspect of this phrase is in its overuse. Like most annoying phrases in this book, once someone latches onto *good with a hammer so he thinks everything is a nail*, they cannot (or will not) let go.

If this is you, your obsession with this phrase (as with all clichés) should trouble you. It certainly troubles the rest of us.

Replacement phrases: No replacement needed; just stop saying it. Additionally, you could go one step further. You could find a second talent of this person who's so good with a hammer.

See also: *Jack of All Trades, Master of None*

30,000-Pound Gorilla

"Dan, I think we'd all like to see a little less grinding and a lot more working."

Grind

If *grind* was only used in business to describe one's tedious workday, then it never would've made the list of the most annoying business phrases you hear today.

Unfortunately, thanks to the crop of ubermotivationalists among us who record daily inspiration from their smartphones while driving (think: a less polished, less famous, though just as annoying Gary Vaynerchuk), we've learned that the only way to succeed at anything is to "rise and *grind*" and that TGIF really means "The *Grind* Includes Friday" and that "I had to *grind* for this view."

Moreover, if you don't *grind* non-stop *24/7/365*, then you can never fully enjoy your life.

This begs the question, of course: If you're always grinding, when do you get a chance to enjoy life?

In the last century, *grind* was preceded by "the" and it most often referred to the struggle to get through one's workday. "The *Grind*" meant "work" and had negative connotations. Today, it still means work; though, work that apparently deserves a medal, a trophy, and a cookie.

We all work, and some work can be a *grind*; though most of us can show up early, do our job, and give our best without telling our network about it *24/7/365*.

As we already learned about with *disruptors*, before social media, the only people who bragged about how hard they were working were those that accomplished the least. We're pretty sure that's also the case with the rise and *grind* crowd at your job today.

Replacement phrases: No replacement phrase needed – just stop saying it; you sound absolutely foolish to the rest of us.

See also: *Crushing It; Go-Getter; Hustle*

"Wow, Petrotto has really let the Search Marketing Guru title go to his head."

Guru

Guru is not so much an annoying phrase as much as it is one in a long list of annoying, douchey, self-bestowed titles and job descriptions today's plebeians (mostly in the technology and digital marketing fields) have chosen to claim.

Guru, along with ninja, warrior, rock star, wizard, czar, evangelist, and even guerrilla now show up on business cards and on LinkedIn profiles to prove to the world these people are not just competent, they're also spiritual (*gurus*), stealthy (ninjas), fierce (warriors), drug-addicted (rock stars), magical (wizards), royal (czars), preachy (evangelists), or even saboteurs (guerrillas).

So, instead of proudly executing your job duties as the Social Media Marketing Coordinator for your company, you claim to be the Social Media *Guru*! Your boss doesn't care because she worries about the important stuff… plus, she already thinks you're kind of weird.

But, of course, nothing says you can really dominate the world of social media more than a stupid title you've bestowed upon yourself. Congratulations; now, no one need give you a raise because you've already given yourself a promotion!

You truly are some special kind of *guru*, aren't you?

Replacement phrases: Pick a job title that describes what it is you really do. This mean, unless people are climbing a mountain to hear your wisdom about posting on Pinterest, you're a coordinator, not a *guru*.

See also: *Disruptor; Thought Leader*

30,000-Pound Gorilla

"I think we've reached the point where we need less growth hacking and more actual growth."

Hack

Back in the day – before the internet – when someone was able to provide a useful shortcut to a task, it was called a shortcut. When they shared a tip on how to reuse something (for example, how to turn empty wine bottles into an ugly, noisy wind chime), it was called a tip. And when they gave you advice on how to move up in your career or build your business, it was called advice.

Today, each of these are known as a *hack*. (Well, at least according to the annoying people at your work they are.)

Usually uttered by hacks, everything has become a *hack*. We kid you not.

There's a *hack* for tying your shoes; there's a *hack* for getting ketchup out of a bottle; and there's a *hack* for reusing wine bottles. Don't believe us? Google this crap.

The same dumb tip you would read about in a crafting book in the 1980s detailing how to turn your empty wine bottles into one of the most disgusting and dangerous windchimes of all time is now available from hundreds of websites as a verifiable life *hack*. (A life *hack* should not to be confused with a growth *hack*; which is the new douchey way to say career or business advice.)

Google "empty wine bottle *hack*" and you'll find dozens of dull and utterly worthless uses for your empty wine bottles. (Which begs the question: Why do so many people have so many empty wine bottles anyway?)

Hack, of course, originated from hacking – as in computer hacking. You know, those nerdy guys holed up in their parents' basements typing away endlessly in an effort to steal your identity, swing elections, destroy the power grid, and end civilization as we know it?

Understanding this makes it all the more bizarre that *hack* has become so widely accepted as a positive thing. We, of course, just find it positively annoying.

Replacement phrases: Shortcut; Tip; Advice

See also: *Action Item*

30,000-Pound Gorilla

"Unfortunately, our Hail Mary was intercepted by the competition and returned for a touchdown."

Hail Mary

A term sports borrowed from Catholicism has been (for decades) overused and misused in business. A *Hail Mary* in sports is a last chance prayer, if you will.

In football, it's a long pass by the trailing team into the end zone as time is running out in a close game. In basketball, it's a near full-court shot as the clock expires by a team down three or fewer points.

In both cases, the *Hail Mary* is the team's last chance to avoid a loss. In business, annoying managers overuse and misuse *Hail Mary* to vaguely explain the action needed to save a deal, keep a good employee from leaving, or get a project back on track.

It's annoying on the surface and annoying in its inability to provide any sort of direction. Saying, "We need to throw a *Hail Mary* on this one," allows weak leaders to feel contributory without actually contributing anything.

It's just their way of shedding their responsibilities and heaping everything onto anyone within earshot.

Oh, and it's their way of saying, "Look at me; I just used a cool sports analogy to prove I'm not just serious, but also seriously hip." Ugh.

Replacement phrases: No replacement needed; just try being a leader and giving your team clear direction and actionable advice.

See also: *Next Level*

30,000-Pound Gorilla

"The boss was right; we just needed to hammer it out."

Hammer it Out

You're close to a deal… there are a couple of points where you and the other side still disagree, but the overall structure is there. What's your next step?

Well, if your annoying manager is involved, he'll tell you exactly what to do next. He'll say, "*Hammer it out.*" Ugh, so annoying.

He tells you this in a self-satisfying way because he believes *hammer it out* is more than a saying, it's a solution. In his mind, hearing it should hit you like epiphany; hearing it should make you feel honored to be working for such genius; hearing it should propel you into a *win-win scenario* – an agreement we all can love.

In his mind, you just need to *hammer it out* because, after all, *it's all in the details.* Double ugh, truly maddening.

Hammer it out is used by those who lack a penchant for the details; those who have ultra-short attention spans; those who lack business acumen. *Hammer it out* is the business equivalent of "go team!" in sports. It also means, "I can't be bothered by such triviality; you handle it!"

It's hollow and directionless; and it implies your boss thinks you're so weak minded you just need a little motivational push from above to successfully complete the task.

Unfortunately, given the weakness of those using *hammer it out*, the replacement phrases are no better; they're just not clichés.

Replacement phrases: Work it out; Come to an agreement; Finalize the details

See also: *Buy-In; Win-Win Scenario*

"To be fair officer, the sign doesn't say it's a hard stop."

Hard Stop

Hard stop is used proudly by the smuggest of the smug in business to let you know they have more important things to do than whatever it is they're doing with you. Just as your conversation begins you'll hear, "I have a *hard stop* in five minutes."

If they feel they can only spare five minutes, why not just say, "I have a meeting in five minutes," or "I have to poop," or "I have the attention span of a gnat, so I can't dedicate more than five minutes to any conversation?"

Because *hard stop* sounds cooler and way more significant.

We mean that. *Hard stop* sounds cool. The first time Steve heard it he was hooked. *Hard stop* is to an adult businessperson as smoking is to a teenager. They know it's wrong, but it just seems really, really cool. So cool, in fact, they can't wait to try it so they can be cool too!

Steve knows… because that was him. Both as the teenage smoker and as the adult telling everyone about his *hard stop*. Man was he cool! Of course, the problem with smoking is that it's so addictive it's nearly impossible to quit.

Steve knows… because it took him years to finally kick the habit.

Uttering *hard stop*, it seems, is more addictive. Steve knows it's wrong. He knows it's annoying. He knows it's not cool, but he can't stop. Steve is embarrassed every time *hard stop* comes out of his mouth, but he still hears himself telling someone about his *hard stop* at least weekly. And even though the shame he feels saying *hard stop* is greater than the shame he felt while smoking, he can't stop.

To be clear, Steve was going to write a bit more on this, but he's at a *hard stop*. Perhaps someone could invent a patch or gum to help people like Steve.

Replacement phrases: I have another meeting/engagement/appointment; I have to poop

See also: *Firewalled*

30,000-Pound Gorilla

"Ackels, I'm afraid the shareholders are going to want to hear more than 'haters gonna hate' to explain the drop in sales."

Haters Gonna Hate

While you'll still hear this adolescent phrase uttered way more in your personal life than in your work life, its slither into business is real… and it must be halted; reversed; eliminated!

The entire concept of haters at work — those who are openly plotting against your success — is mostly an imaginary enemy created to self-motivate those who need such a thing. You know, the ones who tell you how much they *grind* and *hustle*?

Yes, there are those who may want you to fail at your job. These people are petty, jealous douchebags. They're also cowards. They don't openly tell you they want you to fail; they won't say they don't believe in you.

In other words, you don't have haters; you have little people so consumed by their own inadequacies they want everyone to be as miserable as they are. Conversely, those who provide constructive feedback or even openly question your sanity aren't pulling against you; they're most often pulling for you; concerned for your well-being.

When you tell us *haters gonna hate* (or worse, share it in meme), you're telling us you're part paranoid, part professional victim, part immature, part insecure… and all annoying.

Please get some help.

Replacement phrases: No replacement needed; just try getting by without the need for false self-motivation.

See also: *Crushing It*

"Well, he's the best recruiter we've ever had, but all his new hires seem to disappear overnight."

Headhunter

Proudly used by hiring managers everywhere, the word *headhunter* is annoying both in its arrogant overuse and in the complete lack of comprehension of the word's origins. (Oh, and it sounds ridiculous to the rest of us.)

To be blunt, *headhunters* murdered their victims, cut off their heads, then shrunk these heads and displayed them as trophies. To top off this wonderful visual, they also cooked and ate the rest of the body.

"Mommy, I want to be a *headhunter* when I grow up!"

The egotistical overuse in the workplace forgets that true *headhunters* are proactive. They seek out heads. Yet, almost everyone in the business world claiming to be a *headhunter* is really just a passive hiring manager (not even a recruiter by the strictest of definition).

They seek out no one; they merely sit back and sort through the resumes of those seeking employment; those answering an ad.

True *headhunters* pursue heads. They pick up the phone and call the underappreciated vice president at a rival company and offer her a job. They're active, not passive, recruiters of talent.

Of course, if you're an active recruiter (as opposed to a hiring manager) why not just say you're a recruiter instead of using *headhunter*? After all, recruiting is really all you do. No offense.

Replacement phrases: Hiring manager; Recruiter

See also: *Bean Counter*

Unfortunately, after the latest round of layoffs, the company had to depend on Garvin to do all the heavy lifting.

Heavy Lifting

Your annoying boss – as is true with all annoying bosses – believes he's superhuman; he believes he's the most important person at the company; he believes the entire organization would fold without him.

He tells you this on an hourly basis. Not directly, of course; he thinks he's too sly and sophisticated to openly express these thoughts.

He believes his actions and results speak for themselves. Unfortunately for this jerk, he gives himself away with every irritating utterance.

One of his favorite annoying phrases includes *heavy lifting*, as in, "Well, I can't do all the *heavy lifting*."

Of course, he certainly believes he can do all the *heavy lifting* – he's always believed this – however, in this case, he's passively-aggressively asking one of you peons to step up and take some of the load off this overworked superhero.

The funny part about those who claim they cannot do all the *heavy lifting*, is that they never seem to do any of it. They're only good at delegating because they're both egomaniacal and lazy.

A combination, of course, proven to create annoying managers.

Replacement phrases: No replacement needed; just describe the situation in direct terms with no passive-aggressiveness, please.

See also: *Stay in Your Lane*

30,000-Pound Gorilla

"Tucker, your resume is very impressive. Tell me about your experience herding cats."

Herding Cats

Let's agree right up front that no one using this term has ever attempted to herd more than a couple of cats at any one time.

This doesn't mean they can't have an appreciation for the frustration one would encounter *herding cats*, only that because they've never actually done it (or even seen it done), they really should stop saying something "is like *herding cats*" as if the realities, hardships, and results of *herding cats* was so well known.

Moreover, as with so many phrases in this book, *herding cats* is especially annoying given the likelihood that once your manager starts saying it, they'll never stop. Ever.

Every imperfect situation that involves people will become akin to *herding cats*.

Scheduling a meeting becomes like *herding cats*. Getting an agreement on a proposal is like *herding cats*. Putting together a team to tackle a specific issue is just like *herding cats*.

Except, of course, none of these is like *herding cats*.

Additionally, describing any situation as being like *herding cats* is exactly the kind of negative speak you don't want from the leaders in your company.

Herding cats, in reality, would be a pointless attempt at an impossible task.

Anyone can tell you how difficult a job is going to be or where the problems lie, but great leaders find solutions and focus on these. Except in jest, a true leader would never be heard describing any situation as *herding cats*.

Replacement phrases: Stop saying it – it's just negative speak.

See also: *Trying to Boil the Ocean; Ducks in a Row*

30,000-Pound Gorilla

"Caldwell, didn't you get my memo? I want everyone to hit the ground running."

Hit the Ground Running

We get it.

It's an important job, client, or product launch. So important, in fact, that it's critical we get off to a good start; that we ensure we're prepared to begin working toward the goal immediately; that we… dare we say it… *hit the ground running*.

Ugh, so damn annoying.

Truly, why is this even a saying? Is it possible or practical to start furiously running the moment your feet touch the ground? To be prepared to hit the ground running in the morning, for example, wouldn't you need to put your shoes on while you're still in bed? Wouldn't you already need to be showered and dressed for the day?

We have an idea; why don't we simply plan, prepare, and execute? What can we possibly expect to gain if we mindlessly *hit the ground running*?

This phrase is annoying beyond its obvious silliness. Its overuse by the rah-rah crowd of managers – those who mistakenly believe they missed their calling as motivational speakers – multiplies the annoyance factor by at least eleven.

If you work for a manager who always wants to be sure everyone is ready to *hit the ground running*, keep a pair of Brooks on top of a copy of *Runner's World* magazine on your desk. Then, glance at these whenever he asks if you're ready to *hit the ground running*. It can be very cathartic.

Replacement phrases: Be prepared; Be ready

See also: *Pick Up the Ball and Run with It*

30,000-Pound Gorilla

Because he was more of a wrench guy, Roland was never able to hit the nail on the head.

Hit the Nail on the Head

That's the goal, right? We mean, the goal when hammering is to *hit the nail on the head*, isn't it? In fact, isn't this the most common outcome when hammering?

Even the clumsiest carpenter or do-it-yourself handyman can *hit the nail on the head* more often than not, right?

Why then is *hit the nail on the head* such an accomplishment to your annoying manager?

"You *hit the nail on the head* with that one Josh! Great job!"

Seems the bar is set a little too low in your workplace.

Instead of *hit the nail on the head*, why not "ate the sandwich" or "pulled up your own pants?" It seems to us that if hitting a nail as designed is an accomplishment worthy of mention, then so should everything from tying your shoes to washing your hands after peeing.

If *hit the nail on the head* wasn't such an antiquated idiom, we'd think it was the result of the participant trophy culture we've created in the last few decades.

The annoyance factor with this one is multiplied by its overuse and its multiple meanings.

Was Josh correct about something? Did he complete a task properly? Does our annoying boss just like saying *hit the nail on the head*? Do we wish Josh really had a hammer and our manager's head was a nail?

We can dream, can't we?

Replacement phrases: Correct; Complete

See also: *Par for the Course*

Sadly for Koda, his lack of opposable thumbs made it impossible for him to hold hands with the rest of the team on the important projects.

Holding Hands

Despite the spotlight placed on inappropriate behavior in the workplace, some annoying managers insist everyone should be *holding hands*.

"I'll need you two *holding hands* on this one," you'll hear them say.

Holding hands may sound fun and innocent enough, but just try doing it with a stranger… in public… in front of his or her spouse.

Holding hands sounds a little less fun now, doesn't it?

While we all understand our manager is asking us to cooperate or work together on something, we don't understand why she doesn't just say that. Why do the annoying among the leadership ranks continue to speak in irritants?

Why can't we just get through one meeting without being bombarded by assaults on the English language?

Why can't we all just get along… and hold hands for real?

Replacement phrases: Cooperate; Work together

See also: *Get Into Bed*

30,000-Pound Gorilla

"I explained the dangers, but he insisted on seeing firsthand how the sausage is made."

How the Sausage is Made

Apparently – and we write apparently because neither of us has ever witnessed the act of sausage making – no one should ever see *how the sausage is made*.

Why? We don't know; though, we're also pretty sure your annoying manager – the one who overuses this one – doesn't either. You see, he or she has likely never experienced sausage making in the flesh, as it were.

This one's annoying because it's overused, implies something that must be disgusting, and – this one really grates our nerves – it's often uttered by the same manager at different times with completely different meanings.

Give too many details in a presentation or report and you'll hear, "We don't need to know *how the sausage is made*."

Discuss how much transparency to provide a client and the response will be, "Don't let her see *how the sausage is made*."

Attend a breakfast meeting at Denny's and your annoying manager will invariably tell you, "You don't want to know *how the sausage is made*."

Okay… umm… so, sometimes this refers to sausage, sometimes it refers to what we should hide from customers, and sometimes it just refers to the minutiae. Is that it? As annoying as this one is, somehow it makes us want to actually see *how the sausage is made*, doesn't it?

Replacement phrases: Details

See also: *Warts and All*

30,000-Pound Gorilla

DeFacci set himself apart by always showing he was one of the only true hustlers left in the business world.

Hustle

A couple dozen pages ago, you learned about *grind* — a misused word meant to describe the unequalled dedication of most of today's hyper-entrepreneurs (everyone's an entrepreneur today, right?).

Like *grind*, *hustle* tells the world the user is always working; always moving; and always focusing on their goals. Their commitment is so great that it's not enough we simply notice it. No, they're compelled to tell us how much they *hustle*, and how they're always hustling.

But, *hustle* (by itself) is not enough for those who are truly *crushing it*, is it? No; *hustle* must be preceded by an octothorpe to create a hashtag — even when their *hustle* details are shared somewhere other than on social media. (Steve has a colleague who includes *#hustle* as part of his incredibly annoying email signature.)

#hustle tells the world they're unstoppable because they never stop working… never… ever.

Except, of course, to post on social media about how much they're hustling, right?

Here's a hint: People who are truly hustling; truly grinding it out; and truly *crushing it*, don't stop to tell the world about their *hustle*, their *grind*, or how they're *crushing it*. They just do.

Replacement phrases: No replacement phrase needed; just actually *hustle*, and the results will show.

See also: *Crushing It; Grind; Go-Getter*

"I laugh when I think of all the money our competitors are wasting on computers. As I've always said, 'if it ain't broke don't fix it'."

If It Ain't Broke Don't Fix It

Sound advice, we suppose. Unless, of course, if by "fix" we simply mean improve.

No offense, but if you've heard your annoying manager utter this more than once, we're going to peg his or her age at 60+… maybe pushing 70.

Are we stereotyping? Yep. Are we wrong? Nope.

If it ain't broke don't fix it screams both "I'm old" and "I have a crippling fear of change… any change… especially improvements."

Fear of change is a debilitating issue for any manager; and it can spell doom for your company if these managers are near the top of the organizational chart. Believing that *if it an't broke don't fix it* means we're not going to even think about improvements, tweaks, alternatives, etc. until we can declare something is broken. The problem for business, of course, is by the time something is indeed broken, it's often too late to fix.

Instead of poo-pooing change, your annoying manager should embrace it.

Certainly, he'll also want to improve his vocabulary to include more than just those three or four phrases his grandfather overused (and that he can't stop using today).

Unfortunately for you, if this describes your manager, and you dared suggest he open his mind a tad while also bringing his vocabulary into the 21st century, he's likely to respond, "*If it ain't broke don't fix it*."

Therein lies the problem.

Replacement phrases: No replacement needed; uttering this makes you sound like an annoying old fart.

See also: *Reinvent the Wheel*

30,000-Pound Gorilla

"No one impacts the competition quite like Hannan."

Impact

Despite what you'll read in the dictionary, *impact* is a noun; never a verb.

Yes, we're overriding generations of Websters here. We're doing this because, in the workplace, the overuse of *impact* as a verb has become epidemic.

No longer do we change, challenge, effect, grow, or even attack something, someone, or some company. Today, we *impact* it, him, her, or them.

What does that mean? Is it a good thing? Is it a bad thing? We often have no idea… we just know the situation demands we *impact*… and we *impact* now.

Where once your annoying manager would explain how we need to grow sales, today she tells you we need to *impact* sales. Umm, excuse us, but wouldn't reducing sales also be correct if we're only instructed to *impact* them?

Yes, our point exactly! Positive or negative outcomes are only implied when the higher ups demand we *impact* something.

Today, we're asked to *impact* so much in the workplace, we fear we'll never be rid of this annoying usage. Our only hope is to demand clarity when asked to *impact* something. Perhaps this will help the chronically annoying jettison their ear-bleeding need we *impact* everything.

Here's how we'll do it: beginning today, when your boss or coworker uses *impact* as a verb, just ask them to explain what they mean.

For example, your manager says, "We'll need *all hands on deck* to *impact* sales this week."

Just reply as genuinely as possible and with no snark detectable in your tone, "Does this mean you want us to expand or contract sales this week?"

Do this enough times and you'll never hear this boss use *impact* as a verb again… because, of course, you'll be unemployed. No one likes a smartass.

Replacement phrases: Effect; Attack; Grow; Improve

See also: *Incremental Improvement*

30,000-Pound Gorilla

"While only being 30 minutes late does represent an incremental improvement for you; I was hoping your punctuality would improve in larger increments."

Incremental Improvement

This one's annoying for a couple of reasons – one of which is common among most of these sayings. That is, *incremental improvement* is overused by those who use it. It's one of those sayings marginal managers seize and just won't give up. Everything becomes an opportunity for *incremental improvement*.

If that was the only thing annoying about it, *incremental improvement* likely wouldn't have made the cut. Our real problem with this one is that we often have no idea what the speaker's intention is when they use it.

"We made *incremental improvement* this month." Is that good or bad? Is that a lot? A little? More than that, was it incremental enough?

Possibly no saying in business has become more vague than *incremental improvement*. Which is funny, of course, because its meaning should be clear.

Incremental most often means a change along a fixed scale. That is, an increment. A measurable thing.

Improvement, of course, tells us which direction the incremental change occurred.

Used correctly, there would be context accompanying the statement. Perhaps a chart showing the various goals at different increments.

Unfortunately, clarity and content are almost never delivered by those spouting about *incremental improvement*. For us, we're often left wondering if the *incremental improvement* was a good thing or a bad thing.

Think about it; if you're looking for great results, an *incremental improvement* is a disappointment, right? Conversely, if your results have been flat and you make an *incremental improvement*, then that's good, right?

So… telling a group they made an *increment improvement* without context is just confusingly annoying, right?

Stop it.

Replacement phrases: Improvement

See also: *Impact; Move the Needle*

30,000-Pound Gorilla

"Given your analysis of every challenge is 'at the end of the day, it is what it is,' let's go ahead and make this your last day."

It Is What It Is

What *incremental improvement* is to vague, *it is what it is* is to clarity.

So clear, in fact, it borders on imbecilic.

There's never been a truer or more redundant statement ever made in business. Yes, "it" is exactly what "it" is. It is, or it wouldn't be it, would it?

Often such a defeatist notion, this one screams of equal parts passive-aggressive, self-righteous and just plain weak. To those who claim *it is what it is* is somehow an esoteric phrase that attempts to describe the indescribable: it's not.

It is what it is.

When used in business, *it is what it is* is more of an "I give up" or an "I can't do anything about it" resigned response to a negative outcome.

The speaker of this phrase is telling you they are helpless; things are not in their control. Given this, it's beyond time to strike this annoyance from your vocabulary.

Replacement phrases: No replacement phrase needed because… well… *it is what it is*.

See also: *Easier Said Than Done; Are Two Different Things; There's a First Time for Everything*

30,000-Pound Gorilla

"Mr. Urias? Yeah, you'd better get up here. We've got a cart and horse situation."

It's a Cart and Horse Situation

What started as a warning to those getting ahead of themselves or doing things in the wrong order ("don't' put the cart before the horse") has morphed most often into a lazy, throwaway line to indicate the scheduled implementation of a plan is backwards or some of the steps are in the wrong order.

Saying *it's a cart and horse situation* is the annoying manager's way of telling you your strategy is somehow wrong. Without, of course, explaining why he feels this way or what you can do to remedy the situation.

Moreover, by telling you *it's a cart and horse situation*, he's basically saying that only an imbecile like you would try do something so obviously backwards as to put the cart before the horse. After all, even a child knows the cart goes behind the horse.

This saying, by the way, has nothing remotely in common with "it's a chicken and egg thing" (which is annoying, but not annoying enough to make the cut for this book). The chicken/egg comparison relates specifically to the debate about which of two things came first.

When you're dealing with a cart and a horse, there is no debate… *it's a cart and horse situation.*

Replacement phrases: The replacement for this one is to simply explain – in human terms – what you mean. Mangled idioms are annoying, unnecessary, and less effective than using plain language to drive the results you want.

See also: *Go Slow to Go Fast*

"Listen Bledsoe; instead of just saying 'it's all in the details,' perhaps you can give us a few."

It's All in the Details

It's all in the details is uttered by those who don't know the details. They don't know them, of course, because they've never bothered to read them… and they wouldn't understand them if they did read them.

They're dolts – which, unfortunately, is often a prerequisite for most management positions today.

Saying *it's all in the details* is a simple, yet futile attempt at misdirection. Managers who use this one fancy themselves as magicians or puppet masters (or both); and they (wrongly) believe they can fool you and the rest of the team with their words.

Rather than grasping what's happening and helping fashion a strategy, annoying managers are famous for deflecting and procrastinating. *It's all in the details* is the ultimate deflection; and a sure sign you've been right all along: your boss is an idiot.

Replacement phrases: No replacement needed; just learn the details.

See also: *Lost in the Sauce; Devil is in the Detail*

30,000-Pound Gorilla

"Of all people, you'd think he'd know it's more of a cubicle than an office."

It's All Semantics

Semantics – basically the meaning or interpretation of words – is an important linguistic discipline.

On second thought, not so much of a discipline as a study.

Actually, semantics is more of a branch of knowledge than a study, now that we think about it.

Well, to be precise…

Yikes, it looks like we're getting bogged down in the semantics! Of course, according to some annoying managers, *it's all semantics*. To this group, there are no longer any legitimate disagreements because *it's all semantics*.

Truthfully though, it can't all be semantics; sometimes *it is what it is*, right? (Ugh; we are annoying ourselves writing some of these.)

Whenever someone casually throws in *it's all semantics* in a meeting, we want to cringe. Don't get us wrong, we are not anti-semants; it's just that those uttering this phrase often overuse it to explain away every difference of opinion in business.

It's all semantics becomes their catchall category to describe nearly any disagreement about what was said or implied. Hint: It's not all semantics. Most often, it's a very clear misunderstanding by one of the parties that has nothing to do with semantics and everything to do with either speaking clearly or listening attentively.

Semantical discussions were fun in high school, unheard of during Steve's four years in the US Marine Corps, fun again in college, useless in business. If there really are semantical issues in your business, it's likely the cause of some annoying manager using too many of the phrases in this book.

If you are the leader, learn to speak plainly. Ask for exactly what you want, and then test for comprehension. Check in occasionally to ensure everyone is still working toward the same goal and offer your assistance.

If you ever find yourself saying *it's all semantics* to explain any disagreement, find a mirror and take a good look at the real problem. Business, after all, is not hard, it just takes work… and it's almost never semantics.

Replacement phrases: No replacement needed; this one is just wasted breath.

See also: *Literally; Agree to Disagree*

30,000-Pound Gorilla

"Actually, it is rocket surgery."

It's not Rocket Science/It's not Brain Surgery

(We combined these two because their meanings are identical, and they're often interchanged.)

Meant to infer some task or thing is relatively easy to complete or understand (when compared to rocket science or brain surgery), both sayings are now so overused and dated you often feel sorry for those in your office who utter them.

Do they think these hack phrases make them sound hip or smart? Probably. Of course, to the rest of us, they come across as out-of-touch goofballs repeating an annoying phrase that was never hip; never smart.

Both *it's not rocket science* and *it's not brain surgery* are equally annoying; though the most annoying use of these occurs when the clueless jokester at your company combines them into one of two possible phrases.

While both possible combinations of these are decades old and no longer funny, they (like the original phrases) simply will not go away. The combinations are the dreaded "it's not rocket surgery" and the less popular "it's not brain science."

Both are usually followed by a knowing grin and chuckle from the user – as if he just said something so original and clever that everyone will laugh and take note of this exact day and this exact time.

He imagines his coworkers will gather years from now and one of them will say, "Do you remember that time Dick said, 'It's not rocket surgery'? It still makes me smile. What a clever man Dick is – we're lucky to have him on the team."

The reality, of course, is everyone is annoyed by most everything Dick says; therefore, they rarely retain any words he speaks for more than a few seconds.

Our advice? Don't be a Dick.

Replacement phrases: No replacement needed; you're not funny or original.

See also:

30,000-Pound Gorilla

"As you'll see from my resume, jumping from job-to-job every couple of months allowed me to become a Jack of all trades."

Jack of All Trades, Master of None

Jack of all trades, master of none is an insult that's in some way the opposite of *good with a hammer so he thinks everything is a nail*.

In the latter, the insultee is good at something – probably too good.

In the case of *jack of all trades, master of none*, the insultee isn't all that good at anything. Worse, the insultee fancies himself an expert on all things, while the insulter pretty much thinks the insultee is worthless.

The annoyance with this saying comes from both its overuse and its incorrect blanket assumptions.

The longer you work in business, the more you'll find everyone is good at something. Additionally, you can (and should) learn something from everyone you meet – especially at work.

We're well beyond the time to shelve most of the terms and phrases in this book, but getting rid of *jack of all trades, master of none* is long, long overdue.

Those in your business still insulting coworkers, subordinates, or superiors probably need to remember the advice their mothers likely gave them. That is, if you don't have anything nice to say about someone, don't say anything at all.

Replacement phrases: No replacement needed; just try finding the value in everyone. (Now, let's all hug and sing *Kumbaya*.)

See also: *Good with a Hammer (So… Everything is a Nail)*

"Take it from me, that juice is definitely not worth the squeeze."

Juice is not/is Worth the Squeeze

This one is so annoying, so cringe-worthy, it felt weird even typing the title.

Before we dissect the annoyance factor of this one, we need to ask: How many of us are squeezing our own juice from actual citrus? Not something you buy at a juice bar, get from a packet you insert into a machine, or as the result of dumping frozen bits into a juicer; but really squeezing an actual fruit to extract its juice?

The *juice is not/is worth the squeeze* is about as irritating as a business saying can be.

Usually uttered by those wearing the most expensive business suits, the *juice is not/is worth the squeeze* lands on the ears of the listener like a lead weight. It's pompous; and it's expressed solely for appearances.

The *juice is not/is worth the squeeze* screams, "look at me; I'm pretty freaking cool; I learned a new saying that I'm going to beat into the ground like every other hackneyed saying I discover!"

The phrase's meaning is clear: the expected result is or is not worth the effort. Despite its clarity, this saying needs to go; the users need to be shunned or fired (if you have the juice to do that).

Firing an annoying manager? Now that juice would be worth the squeeze, wouldn't it?

Replacement phrases: Worth It; Worthy; Not Worth It; Unworthy

See also: *Could Care Less*

30,000-Pound Gorilla

"Well, if we're good at anything, it's at jumping the shark."

Jumped the Shark

Part of the annoyance factor on this one is created because most users of *jumped the shark* have no idea of its origins. They'll tell you something is past its prime, no longer relevant, gone too far, or on a downslide by explaining how it's *jumped the shark*.

They're pretty sure they're using the phrase correctly, but if quizzed, they'd have no idea the original shark jumper was The Fonz. To someone who was alive in the 1970s (like Steve), this is very annoying.

Moreover, many will assume incorrectly that *jumped the shark* is more about the downslide than the act that caused or marked the beginning of the downslide. They're wrong.

The act of jumping a shark – which Fonzie did early in the fifth season of *Happy Days* – is often the cause of the downslide and always marks the moment when the downslide began.

Petty difference, we know; but you should know by now we can be petty when it comes to business language (and classic television, apparently).

Once Fonzie *jumped the shark* there was no saving the show. It was destined to die a slow death (which it did over the next six seasons). Referring to the act of shark jumping (and not the subsequent demise) is the only proper way to use this term.

In other words, if you can't pinpoint the act that caused something's downturn, it cannot be a *jumped the shark* moment or situation. It's merely an old-fashioned, boring business downturn.

If you believe our strict definition of *jumped the shark* makes its usage incorrect in all but the most improbable of situations, then you read it right. In business, almost no one ever *jumped the shark*… yet, try telling that to the annoying manager who can't stop saying it.

Replacement phrases: Gone too far; On a downturn; No longer relevant

See also: *Shit the Bed*

30,000-Pound Gorilla

"You see, Price; this is what happens when you constantly ask to be looped-in."

Keep Me Looped In

If you've been in the workforce for more than seven minutes, you must agree that the looping in is out of control. In some offices, it's become unstoppable. Everyone is being looped into everything all the time.

Managers are asking for and committing to so much looping in, most of them should be suffering from motion sickness. We know we are.

The irritating bosses barking, "*keep me looped in*" are requesting this with every project, action, goal, issue, customer, and even bathroom break. Truly, if we kept them looped into everything they requested, we'd have little time for actual work.

If this describes you, it's time for you to stop asking others to keep you looped into things and start trying some old-fashioned MBWA (management by walking around). In other words, get off your ass and find out what's really happening by engaging with your team.

The next time you're tempted to utter *keep me looped in*, try saying instead, "Thank you, I'll check with you later on that." It will be appreciated by the harried team trying to manage their looping in commitments and bring you closer to the issues and solutions.

You're welcome.

Replacement phrases: Keep me informed; Let me know where I can help.

See also: *Touch Base; Reach Out*

30,000-Pound Gorilla

"Bennett is a real stickler. He refuses to land the plane on this project unless everyone is in their seats with their seatbelts securely fastened."

Land the Plane

Though heard infrequently (thank goodness), self-important managers and executives will sometimes ask their charges to *land the plane*.

They say this because, well, they're super cool of course.

What they're requesting is not for you to pilot a 747 to safety; they're asking you to complete something – perhaps even take over a task, project, or job someone else failed to successfully complete.

They'll say, "Jane, I need you to *land the plane* on this one."

You'll cringe and throw up a little in your mouth. It's human nature. As much as you'd like to keep from showing your contempt for your boss's pomposity, you can't help it. He's just that damn annoying.

Instead of losing your gig because of an idiom-loving schmuck like this guy, try working in a secret 'eff you' when assigned tasks in this manner.

Steve's favorite is a quick two-finger salute. This is where you put your index and middle fingers together, put them to your head and immediately fire off a quick salute. To be a true 'eff you,' you'll need the salute to travel quickly upward and outward in at least a 45-degree angle.

Don't know what the heck we mean? Practice a few times in the mirror until only you see the contempt. If you feel the need to show more disgust, feel free to add in a "Roger that," with every salute.

You'll feel much better. We write this from experience.

Replacement phrases: Finish; Complete; Take over

See also: *Over the Line*

30,000-Pound Gorilla

"Let me start by saying I think you hired the wrong CEO."

Let Me Start By Saying

Let me start by saying…

No. We refuse to let you start this way! We refuse to let anyone start this way! Just say it dammit!

If you're compelled to start your soliloquies like this, it's important to understand *let me start by saying* often tells the audience a few things.

It tells the audience you're probably an egomaniac. It tells them you probably love your opinion. And, it tells them this is going to take longer than necessary; much longer.

Our annoyance with this unnecessary beginning is tripled when *let me start by saying* is followed by more than a dozen points no one else agrees with. Sometimes it's followed by a poor restating of something someone else in the meeting already uttered.

Just as the words *let me start by saying* are a waste of breath, so too is everything that follows.

Let me start by saying can also be a verbal crutch used by the weak-minded in your company's management ranks.

In these instances, it signifies to everyone listening that there is very little behind the eyes of the speaker. They know they lack the business acumen necessary to do their job, which leads to a lack of confidence in their opinions, which leads them to start everything with *let me start by saying*.

If the latter describes you, *let me start by saying* you should just shut up… people will think you're smarter than you are.

Replacement phrases: No replacement needed; just start by saying what you want to say!

See also: *Goes Without Saying*

30,000-Pound Gorilla

"You're right, we definitely chose the right salesperson to level set the rest of the team."

Level Set

If you were pitching a script in Hollywood, you'd likely put some importance on the backstory. That is, the history, events, and important character information that take place before the first page of your script.

Without a solid backstory, most scripts would wander aimlessly through their 90+ pages.

Understanding the backstory is important for someone considering your script, though it's something the audience of the finished work will likely never know existed – they'll just catch up as the film unfolds.

For some reason, annoying managers often believe the rest of us need to understand every backstory before we can move forward with the work at hand. They'll tell us they want to *level set* everyone before discussing the meat of the project/issue/meeting/opportunity.

Level set is a lazy, annoying cliché; and its usage is growing.

Unfortunately, the most common replacement phrases for this one are equally lazy and even more cliché. For example, get *on the same page* and bring everyone *up to speed* are probably the closest alternatives in meaning to *level set*; yet, both are, of course, equally nauseating.

During your next meeting, instead of feeling compelled to *level set* everyone in the room, try simply telling the story in the present tense (like any good movie), and give your team credit that they are smart enough to catch up.

Replacement phrases: Brief; Provide background

See also: *On the Same Page; Up to Speed; Sync*

30,000-Pound Gorilla

"I'll light a fire under him as soon as it's discovered."

Light a Fire Under

Apparently, some people at your work are so lazy the only way your manager can get them to move is to *light a fire under* them.

Of course, the only managers that need to constantly light fires under their subordinates are the worst kinds of leaders. Most often, they're from the seagull variety of managers. That is, they occasionally fly in, squawk a lot, shit all over everyone, and then fly away.

Yes, we know this conjures up unpleasant imagery; however, it's nothing when compared to the image *light a fire under* someone creates for the literal among us.

Interestingly, these annoying managers don't want to actually burn their subordinates to death when they *light a fire under* them; they just want to singe them a little; get their attention; get them moving.

We get it, if everyone always did what was best for the company, we never would've invented managers. Therefore, if you're a manager, and you always find yourself needing to *light a fire under* someone, then you need a mirror, not a match. The problem is you, not your lazy subordinates.

Here's a novel idea: perhaps you could stop vomiting clichés and start leading.

Odd advice, we know.

Replacement phrases: Motivate; Lead

See also: *Come to Jesus Meeting*

30,000-Pound Gorilla

As with all previous lines he'd drawn in the sand, Drosen said he was serious about this one.

Line in the Sand

When your annoying manager threatens to draw a *line in the sand*, he acts as if he's going to build the Great Wall of China, doesn't he?

It's a hollow threat, of course. It always is.

He's becoming a bit of a blowhard; so, dipping into the bag of worn-out, useless sayings has become his favorite pastime.

While clichés and other tired phrases are annoying on the surface, hollow threats are especially maddening because we know they're hollow. Everyone knows they're hollow. Everyone, that is, except your annoying boss.

Line in the sand is so often uttered as merely hubris with nothing to ever back it up that we cannot help but smile when we hear it. Those who draw a *line in the sand* get their lines crossed; they get their lines trampled; heck, they get their lines blown away by a cool breeze.

There is likely no other phrase meant to make someone sound tough that makes them sound weaker than *line in the sand*. If you're still using *line in the sand* to express how tough you are, please stop; you're making some of us laugh so hard our sides are starting to hurt.

Replacement phrases: Non-negotiable

See also: *Stake in the Ground*

30,000-Pound Gorilla

"When they told me to stop talking or their heads would literally explode, I thought they were speaking figuratively."

Literally

When *literally* is used to mean *literally*, it is *literally* the best choice of words.

Unfortunately, in business, people are *literally* overusing *literally*. And, we do mean *literally*.

Literally is one of those annoying words you hear in the workplace that does not discriminate. That is, you will *literally* hear everyone from the well-meaning, entry-level receptionist to the ineffective CEO *literally* overusing and especially misusing *literally*.

So much so, it will *literally* make your ears bleed. Not really, of course, we were speaking figuratively; yet (like so many annoying souls in your office), we felt the need to overemphasize the effects of the word *literally* on your ears by *literally* misusing it.

While the linguists among you might argue that *literally* can now *literally* be used for emphasis when you don't really mean *literally*, many more of us are purists… and it hurts our ears (figuratively speaking).

Stop it.

Replacement phrases: Most often, there is no replacement needed; just stop saying it and your meaning will be clear. If you're speaking figuratively, say figuratively.

See also: *Under the Bus*

30,000-Pound Gorilla

"Tell me you didn't lose your dentures in the sauce again, Sharon!"

Lost in the Sauce

When we hear someone in business use *lost in the sauce*, we cringe; then we picture a giant pot of marinara on a stove just as something unsavory falls into it. Now, we're slightly nauseous.

Of course, what we're not doing is listening to the annoying hipster who wants his message to be so clear that he muddies it up with idiotic sayings.

This saying is annoying on the surface; however, its rise in recent years has also led to confusion regarding its meaning. Sometimes, you'll hear *lost in the sauce* from the bigmouth in your office referring to a coworker's confusion. Other times, it will come from the mouth of some mid-level manager suffering from severe egomania warning his "inferiors" of an important point that's getting lost in the details.

Either way, it's infuriating. *Lost in the sauce* rolls off their tongues so cleanly (in their minds) they cannot stop saying it.

Suddenly everything starts to get *lost in the sauce*, including the meaning of *lost in the sauce*.

Replacement phrases: Confused; Lost in the details

See also: *Devil is in the Detail; It's All in the Details*

30,000-Pound Gorilla

"We hired Kruger to help us go after more than just the low-hanging fruit."

Low-Hanging Fruit

Simply put, the *low-hanging fruit* are those opportunities you don't need a ladder to harvest. You can easily reach up and pick the *low-hanging fruit* with little to no effort.

Unless your business is picking fruit, describing anything as *low-hanging fruit* makes you sound like an annoying Captain Obvious to most of your subordinates; and Captain Oblivious to the rest.

You're so annoying, in fact, you even chose to use the *low-hanging fruit* of annoying sayings.

Although you delight in your own sense of cunning – and you fancy yourself a genius of creative thinking – you're not even trying! You're too lazy to speak clearly and too lazy to produce your own euphemism for the obvious, quick, or easy opportunities in your business.

Why call everything *low-hanging fruit*? Why not say "potatoes on the ground" or "fat squirrels" or "dead cats?" At least you'd get the rest of us thinking; pique our interest; get us wondering what in the world you're talking about.

Instead, you settle for the mundane, overused, annoying phrases your grandparents used when they weren't quilting a shawl with their belly button lint.

Yes, given so many managers have lost all imagination when it comes to being annoying, we wanted to create a new annoying business phrase: quilting a shawl with your belly button lint. Feel free to use it to mean someone who is mindlessly working on something that is useless and likely to fail.

Replacement phrases: Obvious, quick, or easy opportunities

See also: *Work Smarter, Not Harder*

"Putnam never forgot the day his pee wee football coach told him he'd never make the cut."

Make the Cut

If *make the cut* was used solely as it is when a high school basketball coach posts a list of those selected to the junior varsity team, it never would've made the cut for this book.

Unfortunately for everyone in your workplace, your annoying manager uses it to describe everything they like or dislike.

"Yeah, that sushi last night did not *make the cut*."

"That new accountant sure does *make the cut*."

"I'm not sure, but I don't think our social media campaign will *make the cut*."

Let's see if we have these right: bad sushi, attractive accountant, underperforming marketing? Are we close? Will our analysis *make the cut*? Should we care?

Replacement phrases: Sorry, there are too many possible replacements given this one has taken on so many disparate meanings.

See also: *Pass Muster*

30,000-Pound Gorilla

"Because of Layton's short temper, HR suggested we warn the other employees."

Minefields

The chronically cautious… strike that. The worrywarts among your management team like to warn about *minefields* in your workplace and/or industry.

They lean on hyperbole because they're obsessed with unlikely outcomes; especially the bad ones. Instead of finding the "can" they're the ones who always find the "can't." They're the modern day Eeyores trying to bring the rest of you down with them.

They speak of *minefields* in generic terms without identifying a single real issue or pitfall. Predictably, they're among the most annoying of the annoying managers you deal with.

To be clear, there are no *minefields* in your office. If you really stop to consider it, there really aren't even that many traps, roadblocks, or even potholes. There's just work.

Of course, with work comes good days and bad days; easy projects and hard ones; smooth patches and rough ones. Somehow, we all survive through another week.

If you're smart, you enjoy your weekend; leaving the tribulations of work (and your annoying manager) at the office. While your irritating, gloom-and-doom manager sits quietly in his basement creating non-existent *minefields* in his head.

Crack a beer and chill; you've earned it.

Replacement phrases: Identify the potential issues in specific terms and offer solutions; just stop warning about nondescript *minefields*.

See also: *Double-Edged Sword*

30,000-Pound Gorilla

"Apparently, Number 43 doesn't understand the meaning of mission critical."

Mission Critical

The problem with this saying – and why it's so annoying – is that almost nothing is genuinely *mission critical* in your business.

Mission critical implies the mission will fail if the *mission critical* element is missing or damaged.

First, you likely have no missions in your business. You have strategies, directions, goals, opportunities, and rollouts; none of these are missions and relatively few of the inputs you seek to achieve these are critical. (There's a difference between important and critical… learn it.)

Many of these inputs might be important, but if there is a workaround or the project can go on without perfecting one of these, then none of these are critical.

Mission critical is from the family of annoying phrases that originates from military terminology. At SpaceX, NASA, or in the US Marine Corps, many things are genuinely *mission critical*. Do these perfectly, or people will die.

For most everyone reading this book, nothing in your business is *mission critical*. Of course, this doesn't stop the self-important in your leadership ranks from dubbing everything *mission critical*. Unfortunately, for those reporting to these managers and executives, when everything is *mission critical*, then nothing is.

Replacement phrases: Important

See also: *Where the Rubber Meets the Road*

30,000-Pound Gorilla

"Given our year-to-date results, it's clear none of us will make his or her bonus unless we adopt a strategy that secretly moves the goal posts."

Move the Goalposts

If you haven't figured it out, we despise sports analogies more than any other category of annoying business sayings. They're too easy, too overused, and too dumbed down to matter in business.

Plus, for this one, who the hell ever moved a goalpost in their life? This shouldn't even be a saying!

Goalposts are often cemented into the ground – yards deep – and they're not mobile. Most have never been moved in real life, so why are we accusing others of figuratively doing this?

Move the goalposts refers to those worthless managers who set a target for their team (perhaps, to receive some bonus), and then move the target farther out as their team approaches it.

It's a lousy way to manage and it leads to employee turnover. Worse, it leads to the wrong kind of turnover. Great people leave, good people underachieve, while the bad people stay put.

Interestingly, those annoying managers most prone to sports analogies (like this one) are often the first to move your targets – that is, *move the goalposts*. They're jerks of the first order; and if you find yourself working for one of these jackasses, you need to start looking for a new gig… now.

We've never known a truly bad manager to get better over time; only worse. Moreover, those accusing others of moving the goalposts are most often the biggest culprits of this unreasonable change.

Replacement phrases: Change the goal; Alter the targets

See also: *Paradigm Shift; Change Agent*

30,000-Pound Gorilla

"I guess I should've been specific when I asked Pasquale to move the needle this quarter."

Move the Needle

When you really think about it, *move the needle* is not just annoying; it's actually a fairly odd expression in business.

Since growth is theoretically infinite, very few real measurements important to business success can be tracked using a needle. Where is this needle? Is it on a gauge? Does it stop at some level?

Sure, nuclear power plants and NASA have gauges, but your business?

Graphs? Sure. Charts? Of course. Spreadsheets? Yep. But a gauge? Almost never.

Without a gauge, there is no needle to move. So, why is it the annoying bosses in our lives continually ask us to *move the needle*? Will they accept any needle movement? Isn't moving the needle down (or to the left, we suppose) still moving the needle?

They didn't ask us to grow or improve; only to *move the needle*. Given this, we take it as a free pass to fail when asked to *move the needle*. You should too.

Replacement phrases: Grow; Increase

See also: *Incremental Improvement; Next Level*

30,000-Pound Gorilla

"Unfortunately, we're losing millions every month, and all anyone wants to offer is their two cents."

My Two Cents

Whether included at the beginning of a thought or as a standalone sentence following an opinion, *my two cents* is usually worth substantially less than two cents.

Generally, it's the naysayers in your workplace who will often overuse this one to add some unnecessary passive-aggressiveness to their message. For example, "If we proceed down that path, we're sure to fail. Just *my two cents*."

You don't agree because you never agree – we get it. Adding *my two cents* to your ill-thought-out opinion now makes it clear what value we should place on it. Thank you.

Of course, it's not just the pessimists who annoyingly overuse *my two cents*. The ineffective, impotent managers in the office will include it to amplify their lack of confidence in their own judgement.

For example, "Well, if you want *my two cents*, I think we should move forward with the plan."

Because this sentence is delivered with all the self-assuredness of an eighth-grade boy asking a girl to the Spring Dance, we dismiss this opinion – as we do with all your opinions – and then we move on.

It's just our two cents, but could you grow a pair?

Replacement phrases: My opinion (however, when it's clearly an opinion, adding "my opinion" would be redundant and highlight either your weakness or innate negativity).

See also: *Agree to Disagree*

30,000-Pound Gorilla

"I call it the Net Net. It catches the money you waste buying worthless solutions."

Net-Net

As annoying as it is to the rest of us when you say *net-net*, why stop there? If net is not enough to describe the bottom line, what makes *net-net* the true bottom line?

That's precisely what a few of our colleagues over the years must've thought when they occasionally volunteered the unicorn of annoying biz jargon, net-net-net.

So, why do you say *net-net*? You say it, because *net-net* reveals your self-importance. It tells the rest of us you're a douche. Strike that. It tells the rest of us you're an annoying douche.

While there are bona fide uses for *net-net* in some tiny corners of the business world, there are likely none in yours. Stop saying it.

If you're describing the result of one thing minus or plus another, that's the net. Adding an extra net doesn't make your result any more final.

Final is final, right? Would you say final-final? Would you say end-end? Would you say climax-climax? If you would, we'd say stop-stop.

Replacement phrases: Net; Bottom line

See also: *Currently Now; Total-Total*

30,000-Pound Gorilla

"I'm afraid our demand that even those on the top floor continually take it to the next level is beginning to backfire."

Next Level

If *next level* referred to some known level above the one where you're operating, this phrase would not have made the cut. Unfortunately, your annoying manager never demands, "We need to take it to the *next level*" to refer to some measurable goal.

No, she just means more; better; faster; bigger; further.

Why is this bad? Because it's unnecessarily ambiguous. Seriously, how will we know when we successfully get there? Is *incremental improvement* enough? Not likely, of course.

The *next level*, like tomorrow, never comes. It's air; it's fluff. For some truly annoying people in your industry, it might also be braggadocio.

You know the type: always telling anyone who will listen how they're busy taking it to the *next level* while spending most of their time creating memes for LinkedIn and Facebook to amplify the fact they're, ugh, *crushing it*.

Of course, when your boss discusses the *next level*, she's not just annoying, she's also vague – which can be doubly maddening for you and the rest of the team.

You'd prefer she ask the team, "To turn it up to eleven;" at least this way there would be some clarity in what she's demanding. (Plus, we all appreciate a good *Spinal Tap* reference.)

Replacement phrases: Just define the level and we'll all sleep better at night.

See also: *Give 110%; Incremental Improvement; Take it Up/Down a Notch*

"It's his own fault. When I asked Berna if he could hit his target, he replied 'no problem'. How was I to know he meant 'no... problem'?"

No Problem

Used everywhere all the time, *no problem* is not just a business annoyance; it's a world annoyance.

Of course, we include it here because it's become an incredibly annoying phrase in the workplace; one we need to strike from our business speak.

Meant as a casual, yet still friendly, replacement for "you're welcome," *no problem* now often sounds like the equivalent of answering "whatever."

As in, "Yes, I did that thing for you, but I only did it because I feel I'm forced to do it for you, and your gratitude deserves no real acknowledgement from me, so *no problem*."

Whatever.

Who said it could be a problem? We asked you for something… you delivered… thank you.

When you answer *no problem*, you're implying there could've been a problem. We get that there wasn't one but that's not the point. There was never going to be a problem!

Your dismissive *no problem* makes us want to take back our thank you.

Why not go old school and reply with "you're welcome?" Or, if you feel the need to be with the times – and make us feel even better about asking you for something in the first place – why not go with the Chick-fil-A "my pleasure?"

Either way, we'll walk away appreciating your efforts way more than if you give us a lackadaisical *no problem*. (And don't get us started on those who use *no problem* as a substitute for yes. Ugh.)

Replacement phrases: You're welcome; My pleasure

See also: *Haters Gonna Hate*

30,000-Pound Gorilla

"But it really is my first rodeo."

Not My First Rodeo

Yes… yes, it is.

When you say, "It's *not my first rodeo*," you're signaling to the rest of us that if this was a rodeo, it would indeed be your first rodeo. We hear *not my first rodeo*, and we think, "Not your first rodeo? Bull. You've never competed in a rodeo! In fact, there's a really good chance you've never even been to a rodeo."

When someone tells you, "it's *not my first rodeo*," they're telling you they're not only super cool, but they've got this one; this one is easy because they've *been there, done that*.

The situation, issue, problem, or opportunity you're describing is passé to them; boring, in fact. They're better than the rest of you because they're an experienced bronco buster or steer wrestler or something.

Not my first rodeo is sometimes the annoying coworker's way of expressing how insulted they feel at being asked about their readiness or experience. As if we're never allowed to ask them about such things.

It's also – and this is where it gets really annoying – the egomaniac's way of expressing they are the king of everything; the master of their domain. Basically, the most qualified, experienced, and smartest person in the room.

They're not. They just like to sound cool. Shun them.

Replacement phrases: Experienced; I've seen this before

See also: *Been There, Done That*

30,000-Pound Gorilla

"I know it's good for my diet, but $10 seems like a lot for a Nothing Burger with Nothing Fries."

Nothing Burger

We like burgers. Burgers, as is the case with pizza and nachos, are the kind of food we will always opt for when an establishment claims some famous or special preparation.

Used first by media members and politicians to describe an issue without merit, or (more correctly) without meat. In other words, it's a burger without any meat; a *nothing burger*.

Like many new annoying phrases, this one started out clever and cute, then quickly devolved into maddeningly irritating. Hearing a new saying when it's new is kind of cool; then, suddenly, it's not only not cool, it's beyond unfashionable.

Nothing burger was kind of cool for about a week. Today, its overuse borders on the extreme – at least for those who use it.

If you've not heard a manager describe something as a *nothing burger*, consider yourself lucky… for now. You will indeed hear it… repeatedly… for the rest of your miserable working life.

To us, *nothing burger* feels like one of those annoying phrases the user thinks is too chic to jettison. Once your manager latches onto *nothing burger*, he or she will never let it go. Everything will become a *nothing burger*, including, unfortunately, your desire to hear virtually any other phrase.

Even if this phrase makes your ears bleed, that outcome will just be another *nothing burger* to your boss. We wish *nothing burger* would go the way of #winning or the Pet Rock, but we fear it will be with us forever.

Replacement phrases: Non-issue

See also: *Stay in Your Lane; Optics*

30,000-Pound Gorilla

"Wait, I thought we were the Walmarts of the world!"

Of the World, The (Blanks)

You've heard these comparisons countless times; and perhaps for you, these nonsensical assessments weren't all that annoying.

Well, you just haven't been listening closely enough.

The Googles of the world, the Walmarts of the world, the Amazons of the world. Enough!

First, there is only one Google, one Walmart, one Amazon. To say *the Amazons of the world* means you don't understand a thing about what makes Amazon, Amazon (or Google, Google or Walmart, Walmart).

These companies have no peers – that's one reason these comparisons are annoying.

Though even when your pompous manager or coworker uses a company or person that actually has peers in their comparisons, they almost always miss the mark.

Saying, "*the Burger Kings of the world*," and then making a generalization about fast food, for example, provides you no real insight into the respective industry; and does nothing to move your business forward.

Moreover, it assumes all similar companies or people share the same tactics or strategy or even vision. Most often they do not, of course.

Despite what your manager thinks, shallow comparisons are not perceptive, instinctive, or even intelligent. In fact, they are the opposite; and they provide nothing tangible on which to act.

We know, we've worked with plenty of *the annoying managers of the world*.

Replacement phrases: No replacement needed; be specific with your comparisons – especially when discussing tactics or strategy you want to emulate or avoid.

See also: *Space*

30,000-Pound Gorilla

"Sorry, boss; but I've already got too much on my radar."

On Our Radar

Your business, we are sad to report to your annoying manager, is not like war. In fact, unless your business is controlling air traffic or predicting the weather, there is never anything on your radar.

Of course, because your boss likes to think your industry is so much like war (and he envisions himself a field general), he cannot help himself when he overuses military jargon to describe the mundane.

"Levenson Chemicals is definitely *on our radar*."

Oh, are they? Exactly where? Are they on our six? Are they attacking our flank? Do we need to mobilize the *troops*?

Being aware of threats or opportunities is certainly important for business success. However, overdramatizing these or even simply defaulting to clichéd jargon can dampen, not elevate, the fighting spirit of your *troops*. (Hint: They're not *troops*; they're associates, employees, or team.)

Instead of reaching for the irritating, overused, and often inaccurate phrases, why not speak clearly? Why not just describe what you mean in unmistakable business terms? If Levenson Chemicals is a potential threat, then say this. If Levenson Chemicals is weak, say that.

Telling us a threat or opportunity is *on our radar* only relays your (possible) awareness of it. It does nothing to explain how you expect the team to capitalize on the opportunity or mitigate the threat.

In fact, it doesn't even tell the team whether it's important to focus on whatever it is that's *on our radar*. In every meeting where a manager explains, "Oh yeah, it's *on our radar*," you'll notice the heads in the room nodding as if they understand and agree.

They don't; they're just wishing they'd been called away from yet another worthless meeting.

Replacement phrases: Considering; Aware of; or perhaps just say whatever it is you mean.

See also: *Troops; Mission Critical*

30,000-Pound Gorilla

"Well, now I know why I can't get everyone on the same page; we're not even on the same book!"

On the Same Page

The only time it's okay to utter *on the same page* in business is when you and someone else are reviewing copies of the same document, and you want to be certain you are both referring to the same word, sentence, paragraph, section, or clause.

Are you literally *on the same page*? This doesn't mean you're in agreement, it simply means you're both referencing the same thing.

Annoyingly, when used in business, *on the same page* most often means in agreement. If that's what you're inferring with *on the same page*, then just say in agreement. As in, "I'm hopeful we're in agreement on this proposal."

The problem with most ineffective managers is they use *on the same page* to manufacture agreement where it does not (and probably should not) exist.

"Come on team; let's get *on the same page* with this one!"

In other words, your annoying boss is trying to cajole everyone to agree with his position and/or opinion. He's given up trying to gain agreement based on the merits or facts. Instead, he's reaching for a hackneyed phrase to make your concerns with his position seem trivial.

As if getting everyone *on the same page* was not just the smartest thing to do, but that disagreeing with him was somehow bad for the rest of the team; perhaps even bad for society as a whole.

As always, his position strives for the greater… strike that… greatest good; so, any disagreement on your part means you're not just dumb, you're uncaring. Shame on you! Can't we just get *on the same page* already?

Replacement phrases: In agreement

See also: *Level Set; Up to Speed; Buy-In*

30,000-Pound Gorilla

"I'd fire him, but it turns out his one trick is blackmailing me over a little office romance I had with my assistant."

One-Trick Pony

This annoying insult (like most insults you hear from bosses) is uttered by the overly insecure managers in your life. They feel threatened by a competitor, a peer, or even a junior employee.

They're threatened because this other person is really good — strike that — really, really great at something. So great, in fact, others marvel out loud at the greatness.

To elevate themselves above this superstar, they insist he or she is just a *one-trick pony*. Somehow, this satisfies their insecurities and allows them to get on with their little lives.

Conversely, when we hear *one-trick pony*, we usually think, "Wait, what if it's a pretty freaking cool trick? We mean, a pony that can do a trick — even just one — is a good thing, right? If that trick is making us a pizza or getting us a beer, we'd be more than satisfied with this pony having just one trick."

Wouldn't you?

Replacement phrases: No replacement phrase needed. In fact, stop insulting those better than you; try celebrating, congratulating, and praising them. You'll earn more respect.

See also: *Good with a Hammer; Jack of All Trades, Master of None*

"I'm not sure this is the time or place to open a dialogue, Spaulding."

Open a Dialogue

We get it. Many readers see this one and wonder why it's on the list. Isn't it clear? Isn't it correct?

Yes… and sometimes.

Yes, it's clear; though, it's only sometimes correct. Oh, and in business, it's always pompous.

Everyone understands *open a dialogue* means start a conversation; though this doesn't make it any less annoying. Generally overused to describe proposed meetings with potential partners, *open a dialogue* is only correctly used when it refers to starting a conversation… and, basically, only the first such conversation.

Unfortunately, its meaning has morphed to cover everything from routine meetings to simple information gathering. Moreover, those who overuse this one will even mention they want to *open a dialogue* with those they've spoken to before – including coworkers! (Starting a subsequent conversation with a party would be "reopening" a dialogue, right?)

"Let's be sure we *open a dialogue* with IT on this one." Ugh, we already speak with IT on a daily basis! Don't you simply mean "Be sure to speak with IT?"

Then. Say. That!

By the way, if you actually enjoy coming across as a self-important jerk, be sure to also overuse the excruciatingly painful "dialoguing" to describe what you're doing once you *open a dialogue*.

We'll all hate you that much more.

Replacement phrases: Speak with

See also: *Ping; Touch Base; Connect With*

30,000-Pound Gorilla

"It's pretty clear we need to stop operationalizing everything and start selling something."

Operationalize

Just because a word is in the dictionary doesn't mean it's not annoying when your manager utters it.

Operationalize feels like a bastardization of the English language... because it is... at least when your manager uses it.

Operationalize is verb that simply means to put something into operation. When used in this manner, our ears don't bleed. However, when the boss wants to *operationalize* a team or a department or a project – when that team, department, or project is already in operation – the meaning is muddy, at best.

Is he saying he wants to motivate a team, reorganize a department, or rethink a project?

Who knows? (Probably not even him.)

Sometimes your boss means conceptualize or create; sometimes he means define or build; sometimes he means leverage or scale. Again, who knows?

Like most of the annoying jargon in this book, *operationalize* is one of those words annoying bosses love to appropriate... and never discard. At first, he likely used *operationalize* in the proper context. Then, over time, you heard *operationalize* spewing from his mouth at every turn.

Everything needed to be operationalized. He begins to speak of the need to *operationalize* the breakroom, the phone system, the organizational chart, and the bathrooms! In fact, nothing is beyond the need for operationalization – even those things running smoothly.

Perhaps, we'll argue, it's time to *operationalize* common sense speech from our leaders.

We could all live happier with that usage, right?

Replacement phrases: If you mean *operationalize*, then okay; otherwise, say what you mean!

See also: *Action Item*

30,000-Pound Gorilla

"Yeah, sales are way down, but the optics have never been better!"

Optics

There are no *optics* worse than saying "the *optics*" to describe how something is perceived.

First used in politics, now managers (and especially executives) everywhere are suddenly concerned with the *optics* of every situation, action, or event.

"I don't like the *optics*."

Yeah? Well, we don't like the word *optics*! If someone is so concerned about perception, you'd think they'd understand how annoying they sound when lamenting about the *optics*.

Yes, it takes more words to utter an alternative like, "how this looks" or "how this will be perceived," but that's not the point. The *optics* are bad when you choose *optics*. You sound like a smug twit.

Of course, if your goal is to sound like a smug twit, then we guess the *optics* are spot on… keep saying it.

Replacement phrases: Perceived; Perception

See also: *Nothing Burger*

30,000-Pound Gorilla

"When I asked if you had time for lunch and you said you were 'out-of-pocket', I thought that meant you were paying for it!"

Out of Pocket

Somehow, someway we've managed to morph the meaning of paying for something yourself into describing one's unavailability.

We blame laziness. Laziness in business language and laziness in the average manager.

Out of pocket once defined (and should to this day) the act of paying for something without the use of company (or insurance company) funds. Today – at least for the most annoying in your office – it means "I'm unavailable."

Ugh; exasperating.

Explaining that you're *out of pocket* when we are trying to schedule a meeting with you tells us you're an idiot who doesn't understand the English language. You're not *out of pocket*. You might be out of the country; out of the office; out of your freaking mind – but, and this we're certain of, you are not *out of pocket*.

Out of pocket should certainly beg the question, "Which pocket?"

Truthfully however, diving into this one any deeper gives us a headache. Please, for the love of human decency, stop saying *out of pocket* to describe your unavailability; it's not even close to what you mean.

Replacement phrases: Unavailable; Out of the office

See also: *Could Care Less*

30,000-Pound Gorilla

"While you did bring this one over the line, you were overbudget. Not to mention you're overcompensated, overemotional, and overbearing; so, I'm going to have to let you go."

Over the Line

Ah, another sports term used in business. Is there anything more cliché? Lazier? More annoying?

Doubtful.

Over the line, as in, "I need you to take this one *over the line*," is a lame, rah-rah attempt by the weakest of weak managers out there to motivate you by regurgitating something they heard their junior varsity football coach say decades ago.

Oh, how the inadequate among us miss those glory days.

Unable to actually hold people accountable, drive results, or deliver anything close to real leadership, the worst managers in our midst resort to hackneyed sports analogies and phrases in some feeble attempt to persuade their charges to do more… to win, if you will.

Using *over the line* to describe a successful outcome is, well, *over the line*… the annoying line, anyway.

Replacement phrases: Finish; Complete

See also: *Pick Up the Ball and Run with It*

30,000-Pound Gorilla

"It's really my fault Walters was stealing computers. I'm the one who asked him to take ownership of IT."

Ownership

For decades – perhaps even centuries – people at work had tasks and duties. Suddenly, and without any warning, they found themselves with *ownership*. Except, of course, they don't really have *ownership*, do they?

Ownership implies equity. That is, if you have *ownership* in something and that something makes money, then you get your share of the money, right?

Unfortunately in business today, *ownership* means nothing. Actually, it means less than nothing. If your jerk manager gives you *ownership* of a project, she's giving you all the responsibility with none of the rewards.

Less. Than. Nothing.

Ownership is a trap; an annoying trap, at that. Getting *ownership* of something is like getting a title instead of a raise. (See the *Cheers* episode "Our Hourly Bread" Season 6, Episode 21 for what this looks like in real life.)

Ownership in your office is meaningless and it doesn't help pay the bills.

"I need you to take *ownership* of that project," spouts the annoying manager.

"I need you to be responsible for the failure of that project, while I take all the credit if it succeeds," hears the average subordinate.

If you're merely referring to a task, say that. If you want someone to be responsible for something, say that. If you're designating someone as the liaison between departments on a project, then ask them to be the liaison.

Simple, right? Yeah… we won't be holding our breath for that to happen.

Replacement phrases: Responsibility; Task; Liaison

See also: *Under the Bus*

30,000-Pound Gorilla

"I wish Mr. Kain would work as hard at growing sales as he does on his golf game. Of course, that's just par for the course."

Par for the Course

The only thing that's *par for the course* in your workplace is your annoying manager's consistent and constant overuse of sports metaphors. This one would be annoying enough if it was just used by the weekend golfers at your job. Unfortunately, *par for the course* slips too easily off the tongues of even those who've never swung a club.

The meaning is clear. That is, some person, some department, some customer, or some competitor did exactly what was expected.

Water being wet is *par for the course*. The sun rising in the east is *par for the course*. Your manager leaning heavily on ear-bleeding jargon is *par for the course*.

Certainly, this begs the question: When something occurs as expected, is it worth mentioning?

Perhaps.

Though, if it is worth mentioning, shouldn't we hear more than just a dismissive, "Well, that's *par for the course*?"

If only.

Replacement phrases: Expected

See also: *Tee it Up*

30,000-Pound Gorilla

"See, all we needed was a paradigm shift."

Paradigm Shift

Excuse the inappropriate (and oh so annoying) analogy, but *paradigm shift* is the crack cocaine of annoying phrases. That is, pretty much after one use you're hooked.

Let *paradigm shift* come out of your mouth just once, and you'll find yourself addicted to the soothing and self-satisfying way it rolls off your tongue. You'll immediately feel more intelligent; savvier, if you will, with a business acumen like no other.

Unfortunately, like all illicit drugs, the high you get from uttering *paradigm shift* will wear off all too quickly. You'll need to say it again. And again. And again.

Ultimately, you'll find yourself chasing that first high – a high that will never be repeated as your body adjusts over time. In a cruel twist, your body conducts its own *paradigm shift*.

While the term is often an accurate representation of what happened or needs to happen in your business, this doesn't make its use any less annoying.

Paradigm shift (which basically refers to a fundamental change in approach, understanding, or thinking) has become so overused in business it's lost its meaning.

To your annoying manager, everything is or requires a *paradigm shift*. From changing how you prepare for a product launch to moving someone's lunch hour back thirty minutes; everything in your business now demands a *paradigm shift*.

Except, unfortunately, your manager's overuse of annoying jargon.

Replacement phrases: Change

See also: *Disruptor; Game Changer*

30,000-Pound Gorilla

"Passing muster was sure a lot easier before they hired Master Sergeant Roberts to lead the team."

Pass Muster

Yes, we realize we just referenced the television series *Cheers* a couple of annoying phrases ago; however, if you've ever watched "The Peterson Principle" (Season 4, Episode 18), you probably get a smile on your face every time your annoying (and likely octogenarian) boss uses the most outdated phrase available today.

In this episode, Norm (he with the most well-known butt-on-a-barstool in television history) reports he lost a promotion because his wife Vera didn't *pass muster* when having lunch with the other company wives.

To this, Woody famously adds, "Well maybe she couldn't reach it."

Brilliant; and something that crosses our minds whenever we hear someone use *pass muster* in a business setting. For us, remembering this Woody-ism is one of those little things you should have in your head that can make the normally excruciating workday seem brighter; more cheerful; even downright funny.

The term *pass muster* should be stricken from the business lexicon not just because it's annoying, but because it's a centuries-old military saying that holds little meaning in today's business environment.

Norm used it correctly. In that, he meant Vera didn't pass inspection. For those who use it in your workplace, *pass muster* can mean everything from simply submitting a report on time to the success or failure of an entire project.

If your boss ever says someone didn't *pass muster* on a given task, be sure to add, "Well, maybe she couldn't reach it."

If you do this in your head, you'll smile. If you do this out loud, you'll smile, and your coworkers will chuckle. Your boss? Who cares? He's stuck somewhere in the 1600s.

Replacement phrases: Pass inspection; Succeed; Fail

See also: *Cut the Mustard*

30,000-Pound Gorilla

"The bad part about going to all-you-can-eat venison night, is it's going to take me a week to pass that buck."

Pass the Buck

Pass the buck basically means to avoid responsibility (generally for some failure) by putting the accountability or blame for something on someone else.

To be clear, this one is not all that annoying… except when the person using *pass the buck* to describe someone else's avoidance of accountability is the King or Queen of buck passing.

Unfortunately, this is the reality in many businesses. You know to whom we're referring: that oaf manager who never takes responsibility; nothing is ever his fault.

Working with that guy would be annoying enough if he wasn't also the most likely accuser of others not taking responsibility. He'll exclaim how, "Joe is just trying to *pass the buck*," in instances where the annoying manager (and not Joe) was the primary catalyst of whatever issues occurred.

Of course, most humans (and especially managers) are wired to avoid taking blame. This is not an excuse; just an observation. Understanding this, we have an idea: why not get beyond the blame game in your workplace and start finding ways to succeed?

Crazy thought, we know.

Replacement phrases: No replacement needed; try to rise above the blame game (it will be great for your career).

See also: *Under the Bus*

30,000-Pound Gorilla

After the pool incident, Frenter was never again invited to a company party.

Pee in Your Pool

The distasteful visual *pee in your pool* conjures up should be reason enough to ban it from your annoying arsenal of workplace phrases.

Oh, you don't use this one? Then you must not be a business consultant. Most often used by outside consultants to mollify in advance the hurt feelings of managers whose departments they're evaluating, *pee in your pool* describes what could happen if the consultant wasn't such a good guy.

It's likely a requirement – perhaps something they teach in consultants' school – for every business consultant to explain within the first few minutes of meeting the managers – the very ones they're going to eviscerate in their final report – to utter, "Don't worry, I'm not here to *pee in your pool*."

To be sure, when a consultant tells you he's not here to *pee in your pool*, he's telling the truth.

He's not here to pee in it. He's here to drain it, take a giant crap in it, and then fill it with concrete.

"I'm not here to *pee in your pool*" is just one in a long list of life's known lies like "the check's in the mail" and "I'll still love you in the morning."

When you hear it, expect the worst… and stay out of the pool.

Replacement phrases: Be disruptive; Cause a disruption

See also: *Baby is Ugly*

30,000-Pound Gorilla

"I can't believe she's holding this meeting without the IT piece."

Piece, The (Blank)

You've heard it and it made you cringe. Just as the meeting was about to end, some annoying coworker or manager couldn't help herself, "Wait, we haven't addressed *the logistics piece* yet."

Ugh.

Not only was this worthless meeting about to conclude, but now someone has initiated what we like to call *the blank piece* challenge.

Almost immediately after we learn we need to discuss *the logistics piece*, someone else chimes in about *the IT piece*… then *the billing piece*… then *the customer service piece*… then… you get it.

They. Won't. Shut. Up.

Everything is now in flux because everything is now a piece deserving its own extended discussion.

The blank piece is an odd phenomenon among annoying business phrases. Unlike most terms in this book, this one is like the flu. It comes into the office; spreads quickly; infects nearly everyone; then disappears for months.

That is, until someone feels there's been too little attention being paid to *the admin piece*… then *the sales piece*… then… Ugh! Enough about the piece!

Replacement phrases: Strike "the" and "piece" from this saying and you'll be fine.

See also: *Silos*

30,000-Pound Gorilla

"I suppose when I told him to 'pick up the ball and run with it' I should've been more specific about the direction I wanted him to run."

Pick Up the Ball and Run with It

Often, annoying jargon is just a lazy way to say something. For example, it takes fewer syllables to say "*optics*" than "how something is perceived."

Not this one. This one is especially and unnecessarily verbose given its meaning.

Like most sports phrases shoehorned into your business life, *pick up the ball and run with it* is usually uttered by the rah-rah manager set – those who put way more faith in hollow motivation than on actual leadership.

Of course, your shallow supervisor just wants you to take control of something – perhaps an important project – and, given this, you should be honored. Unfortunately, when he gives you that shit-eating grin and then asks you to *pick up the ball and run with it*, you're pretty sure you'd rather puke at this moment.

There is no honor in being spoken to like a second-string junior varsity football player who might fall for this kind of inane inspiration.

Might… as even high school sophomores are more sophisticated than your boob of a manager.

Replacement phrases: Take over; Take control

See also: *Over the Line*

30,000-Pound Gorilla

"All I heard was 'ping me' and then a loud thwack."

Ping

Quick quiz: In your office, *ping* is: (A) The brand of golf clubs your boss uses; (B) The sound you hear when the elevator reaches your floor; (C) One half of the name of the paddle-and-ball game in the breakroom; (D) None of the above.

If you answered (D), you're correct.

Since the dawn of email – and especially once texting became ubiquitous – *ping* has become one of the most annoying monosyllabic words you'll hear in the workplace.

No longer satisfied to merely contact someone, we must now *ping* them. Where we once asked someone to call us, we now request they *ping* us.

Ping, you may not know, has some correct usage when it comes to technology. For example, computers and/or servers on the same network will *ping* each other (and get a return signal) to ensure they are in working order (and/or to test the speed of the network).

That's where the correct business usage ends, and the annoyance begins.

When you're asked to *ping* someone, you're not expected to check their vitals (are they alive?) or test how fast they respond. You're expected, merely, to contact them.

We latched onto *ping* (yes, we've caught ourselves saying it way too often) because, simply put, we once thought it sounded hip, and we're lazy. Just because we say it, doesn't make it any less annoying when others do.

Steve's problem is that he knows it's annoying and he hates himself the second it leaves his lips – he just can't stop himself. Of course, the first step toward solving any issue is admitting you have a problem; so, here goes.

"My name is Steve…"

"Hi Steve!"

"… and, I'm a pingaholic."

(If you found that exchange insensitive to people with real problems, *ping* Steve and he'll try to produce a better ending for this one in future editions.)

Replacement phrases: Contact; Call; Email; Text

See also: *Connect With*

"Well, I'm glad someone at this table is ready to play ball."

Play Ball

Though not used as much in business today as in the past, this one is still annoying when you hear someone say it… and fairly sinister when it's said to you.

The inference your sleazy boss is making when he asks you to *play ball* is for you to "look the other way and just go along with the rest of the team on this one." In other words, don't do what's right, just do what's best for all concerned.

Of course, not every use of *play ball* in business is intended to separate someone from their moral compass. Sometimes, you'll hear *play ball* when one of the extra lazy among the management ranks is inquiring about an agreement with a potential customer or partner.

"Do you think they'll *play ball?*"

"Umm, no. We think they'll sign the contract, but since this isn't a freaking game, it's doubtful they'll *play ball*. Of course, if they don't sign the agreement, it's probably because you sound like a character from *Mad Men*. Now, come join the rest of us in the twenty-first century, please."

Replacement phrases: Agree; Go along with

See also: *Team Player*

30,000-Pound Gorilla

"You weren't kidding when you said your team came to play hardball."

Play Hardball

When an annoying manager has tried (in their mind) everything they can to get someone to agree, conform, perform, or obey, they tell you it's time to *play hardball*.

Ooh, scary. Please, don't *play hardball* with him, someone might get hurt!

While there are certainly times when we need to get tougher with a competitor, customer, or coworker, the idea that your boss is going to *play hardball* with someone should be smile-inducing for you.

It's always been for us. Of course, just because hearing *play hardball* makes us chuckle inside doesn't make it any less annoying.

Sure, this phrase is annoying because it's a sports analogy, but that's not even the half of it. *Play hardball* is so often such an empty threat it reveals how impotent and feckless the speaker is.

Primarily, *play hardball* is annoying because it's meaningless.

Play hardball? Who do you think you're fooling? What are you going to do? Grit your teeth; furrow your brow; make that really mean face?

As we wrote earlier: Ooh, scary.

Replacement phrases: Get tough

See also: *Come to Jesus Meeting; Line in the Sand*

That day Chad took the game of Phone Tag a bit too far.

Playing Phone Tag

Stay with us here, Gen Z.

You call someone using a telephone and leave a voicemail.

They call you back and leave a voicemail.

You call them back and reach their voicemail. You are said to be *playing phone tag*.

We understand the concepts of making a phone call and leaving a voicemail seem quite foreign to Gen Z's, but trust us, people still do these things today.

Playing phone tag – when first uttered – was a cute way to relieve the frustration of trying repeatedly to reach someone.

Today, it's just annoying. Today, it's a lazy way of telling someone you're incompetent. Today, when your boss asks you if you reached customer XYZ and you reply you're *playing phone tag*, you're lying.

Perhaps you called once… perhaps.

In reality, you just want to get your boss off your back; you want to be perceived as someone doing their job without actually having to do it. Most people who tell you they're *playing phone tag* are lying; though all who say it are annoying.

Tag, in its purest form, is a playground game involving a group of children. In our experience, to be enjoyable for more than a couple of minutes, tag generally requires at least five or six kids. While the game of tag can be played by just two people, it almost never is… or, not for very long.

Replacement phrases: Left a voicemail/message

See also: *Ping*

30,000-Pound Gorilla

Raines took particular pride in always being the top point person in the company.

Point Person

We know what you're thinking. Wait, why is this one on the list? Isn't it used correctly?

Kind of.

In fact, isn't it the proper way to refer to someone who is the liaison, coordinator, lead, or source of information for a project, department, or prospect?

Perhaps.

Okay, then what gives? Why is this one on the list?

Point person made the cut for three reasons. First, it's the people who say it. Second, it's the way they say it. Third, it's our book and we wanted it in.

When you write your book of annoying business jargon you can leave *point person* out, 'kay?

Unless your business is moving military hardware behind enemy lines, there's no reason for your manager to go all "war room" as he gesticulates like he's guiding a plane onto an aircraft carrier while barking, "Troutwine, you're the *point person* on this one!"

Wait… come to think of it, we guess there are four reasons it's annoying. *Point person* is also irritating given its unclear meaning.

Is the *point person* the one in charge of the project or just the main point of contact? There is a difference, after all.

Generally speaking, point of contact (not quite annoying enough to make this list) is most often the correct way to designate someone as the *point person*. To be clear, point of contact almost made the cut because its usage is inching toward the abbreviations POC and SPOC.

So, while point of contact is not as annoying as *point person*, it could be. Just start saying P-O-C instead of *point person*. Of course, if you want to go the extra annoying mile, use S-P-O-C in place of single point of contact when referring to the *point person*.

Feel like being the most annoying manager on the planet? Pronounce these "pock" and "spock" instead of saying the letters. Congratulations; you've now graduated to complete imbecile.

Replacement phrases: Liaison; Coordinator; Information source; Point of contact

See also: *Run Interference*

30,000-Pound Gorilla

"Sorry, but my boss wants a postmortem of this meeting."

Postmortem

Latin for "after death," the usage of *postmortem* is clear and correct when uttered in the morgue (as in *postmortem* examination; a.k.a. autopsy).

When your manager asks you to give him a *postmortem* of your recent client meeting, you only wish he was referring to an autopsy.

Of course, he's simply asking for a report of what happened and where the relationship is headed. Why he doesn't just ask for a report should be as puzzling as it is annoying.

Our level of annoyance is high with this one because it checks off nearly every box in our imaginary annoying phrases test.

Overused? Check.

Unnecessary? Check.

Better replacement with fewer syllables? Check.

Military, police, or medical term hijacked and bastardized in business? Check.

Uttered to make the manager seem hip and cool? Check.

Non-English term your manager couldn't translate if his life depended on it? Check.

Sports analogy? … Okay, six out of seven – that's still pretty freaking annoying.

Replacement phrases: Report

See also: *Tear Down, The*

30,000-Pound Gorilla

"Apparently, we were at the correct price point, just not the right price."

Price Point

At first glance this one seems fairly innocuous; practical, if you will. Some readers may even defend *price point* as necessary.

It's not practical or necessary; *price point* is just the opposite. It's impractical and above all else, wholly unnecessary.

Impractical, in that adding "point" to the word "price" somehow magically makes it mean more than simply price.

Offering your goods or services at the right price is not enough for your annoying manager; they need your company's products to be at the correct *price point*.

What's the difference? There is no difference, except that in the mind of the user, *price point* displays some non-existent business acumen. Being correctly priced is the goal. Adding an extra word is unnecessary; which is precisely why it's annoying.

Why not simply say price?

If you insist *price point* has a more exact meaning, try removing "point" from every instance where you believe you must use both words.

Go ahead, we'll wait.

There, now don't you feel better? We know the rest of us will. You're welcome.

Replacement phrases: Price

See also: *Game Plan*

30,000-Pound Gorilla

"On the one hand, I appreciate an employee who can pull himself up by his bootstraps. On the other hand, I'm not sure he's going to get much done in there."

Pull Yourself Up by Your Bootstraps

If you hear this one, do the speaker a favor and check his pulse. Chances are he's very near death – or, at least well beyond the mandatory retirement age at most companies.

Pull yourself up by your bootstraps was a last-minute addition and would not have been included if Steve hadn't personally heard it uttered by a senior (in more ways that one) manager of an automotive dealer group while we were finishing this book.

When the manager said it, Steve did a true doubletake. "Did I just hear what I think I heard? Quick, someone get me a calendar, I need to verify we're in the twenty-first century!"

After the phrase sunk in, Steve realized this guy had probably been using it for nearly five decades. Of course, now that this manager was dealing with Gen Z and Millennial workers, he likely felt the need to dust it off and add it back to his arsenal of annoying terminology.

Lucky us. (Well, lucky us, as we now get a chance to overanalyze this irritating phrase.)

When you give this one any thought, it hurts your brain. We know what bootstraps are and we also understand a tad about physics. So… how in the heck did this ever become a saying? Pulling upward on your own bootstraps does nothing once your boots are firmly on your feet. You cannot physically *pull yourself up by your bootstraps*.

Certainly, if someone else pulled on your bootstraps – provided he or she was strong enough – you could be lifted off the ground.

What part of "Yippee, look at me! I'm seven inches off the ground because these two big guys are pulling on my bootstraps!" says success or accomplishment? We give up.

If there's any good news, it's the fact that this is one annoying phrase you probably won't be hearing much in the future. RIP.

Replacement phrases: No replacement needed… at least not from this century.

See also: *Pass Muster; Go-Getter; Soup to Nuts*

"Our research shows the addressable market for envelope-pushing bots is upwards of one billion dollars annually."

Push the Envelope

An aviation term essentially meaning "to go beyond the established boundaries," *push the envelope* has become a favorite among annoying managers of the rah-rah variety.

Instead of leading, these dolts believe they can get more out of their respective teams with hollow jargon and the occasional pep talk. They'll ask their charges to *push the envelope* where no envelope exists. That is, no real boundaries have been established… they just want more… of something; and they think they can achieve this through words.

Of course, employees everywhere respond better to clear direction; but, that's not their concern.

Annoying managers, by their nature, are incapable of clarity… that's what makes them so damn annoying.

Replacement phrases: No replacement needed; just tell us specifically what you want, 'kay?

See also: *Give 110%; Work Smarter not Harder*

30,000-Pound Gorilla

After Glen continued to ask for a raise, George decided it was best to put a pin in it.

Put a Pin in It

Let's be clear: If you're prone to telling others to *put a pin in it*, the rest of us want you to put a sock in it. You might possibly be the most annoying manager of all time. Not because *put a pin in it* is all that annoying – it's not… it's actually a little sad, in fact.

Some of us feel sorry for you. You're wholly uncreative, and you're likely the worst kind of manager. You fancy yourself a great motivator; a top facilitator; a leader of the highest order.

Unfortunately, you're more than a bit out of touch; you're… you're predictable.

Today, for whatever reason, you're hooked on *put a pin in it*, when what you really want to say is, "Let's hold that topic for now."

Strike that. You like to utter *put a pin in it* even when you just mean wait or let's think about it. You can't help yourself, and we get it.

Our point is this: If something is important enough to discuss later, why isn't it important enough for now? Either explore the topic or forget it.

Putting it off tells the rest of us it's not that important, is it? I'd suggest you find a way to stop saying this and find a way to tackle important subjects as they're raised. Of course, you'd just reply that we should put a pin in that idea.

Replacement phrases: Table that

See also: *Put It on the Back Burner*

30,000-Pound Gorilla

"I suppose we should've told Simmons how long we needed him to wait on the back burner."

Put It on the Back Burner

Back-to-back sayings that essentially mean the same thing? Yep… makes you feel kind of blessed, doesn't it?

Even with the influx of cooking (and eating) shows on cable, Netflix, and the interwebs, there's no excuse for sending anything to any other burner in your workplace. Unless, of course, your workplace is a restaurant or food truck.

While the annoying *put a pin in it* tries to convey that an issue is important enough to discuss later (just not right now), this one tells you your issue is a nonissue; worthless; fuhgeddaboudit; *put it on the back burner*.

Of course, the annoying manager who utters this one cannot cook and has no idea that some part of tonight's dinner – an important part, though one that doesn't need constant attention – just needs to be moved to the back burner for now (somewhere other than the front burner where the cook's real attention is required).

This and its overuse are the reasons *put it on the back burner* is annoying.

If you feel something is unworthy of attention, just say so. Telling someone they should *put it on the back burner* is a cop-out; it's lazy; it's weak. Step up and be a leader. We guarantee you'll earn more respect than you will living the milquetoast existence you enjoy today.

Replacement phrases: Drop it

See also: *Put a Pin in It*

30,000-Pound Gorilla

From the day Fitch began putting out fires, productivity ground to a halt.

Putting Out Fires

For those annoying, self-important managers who envision their name should always be followed by a "hashtag hero" (#hero), it may come as a shock that we all know they've never actually put out so much as a trash can fire.

In fact, there's a good chance they've never even had to remove a smoldering bag of popcorn from the microwave in the office breakroom. Despite this, these folks cannot seem to stop telling you how they've been *putting out fires* all day; all week; all month.

Ugh.

Unless you're a member of the Pittsfield (Massachusetts) Fire Department Local 2647, what you do in your business has nothing to do with *putting out fires*, and everything to do with wiping noses and asses.

Yes, we said it.

Instead of telling everyone you've been *putting out fires* all week, how about you tell them something closer to the truth? How about you explain how you've been wiping noses and asses all week?

Not such a hashtag hero now, are you fella?

Replacement phrases: Handling issues; Wiping asses

See also: *Herding Cats*

"I think I have the answer to stopping underage drinking: raise the bar."

Raise the Bar

If *raise the bar* was only used to describe the deliberate act of increasing a goal or target (as it's used in sports), it likely wouldn't have made the final cut for this book.

Unfortunately, many of the irritating types in your workplace like to utter *raise the bar* as a pseudo-motivational attempt to get more production out of their teams.

"We need to *raise the bar* this month!"

Do we? Or, more likely, do you need to *raise the bar* on leadership?

Others annoyingly use *raise the bar* to explain a product or service improvement made by their company or the competition.

"Boy, Ford is really going to *raise the bar* with their new F-150."

Both instances are annoying in their vagueness and in their overuse. What bar? How high was it raised?

At least in sports (and when setting goals in the workplace) the previous and current bar placements are known and measurable.

To *raise the bar* in the literal sense should certainly be referred to in this manner. When the bar was and is invisible, raising it has no meaning – except to mean the person annoyingly asking us to *raise the bar* is an idiot.

Replacement phrases: Increase the goal; Outperform; Over-deliver

See also: *Next Level*

30,000-Pound Gorilla

"I'm serious about only hiring salespeople capable of reaching out to our most distant clients."

Reaching Out

Stop, you're scaring us.

In the current state of virtually everything being inappropriate, forgive us if we don't want you *reaching out*. It's creepy… and, of course, annoying.

What Neil Diamond innocently shared in 1969 – that is, "Hands, touching hands. *Reaching out*, touching me, touching you" – would get you fired in today's workplace.

Let's not only stop with the *reaching out*, let's stop telling others this is what we're doing!

We've all read the email or heard the voicemail: "Hey Steve, it's Gibby. I'm just *reaching out* to…"

Stop! You're reaching out to what? To grope me? To touch me in a dirty place? To make me feel in need of a shower?

Okay, perhaps we're taking this a bit too far, but you must admit this one is just an odd saying. It's creepy and annoying today; but even in its infancy, we're pretty sure it sounded strange to most people.

It always did to us.

Replacement phrases: Contacting

See also: *Connect With*

30,000-Pound Gorilla

"There's nothing to worry about, those guys are just trying to reinvent the wheel."

Reinvent the Wheel

While those in the workplace who waste effort trying to create something that's already been created can be annoying, they're not nearly as annoying as those who constantly chastise everyone with "We don't need to *reinvent the wheel* here."

No, we suppose we don't. Moreover, we'll argue we don't need to keep saying *reinvent the wheel* to cover virtually any improvement effort at work with which you disagree.

Of course, since you've made it your go-to catchphrase, you've accused others of trying to *reinvent the wheel* when they're merely attempting to advance some process in need of an upgrade.

Continuous process improvement is a real thing for successful companies.

To those who spend their days accusing everyone at work of trying to *reinvent the wheel*, we retort "successful companies *reinvent the wheel* every chance they get!"

Of course, normal people understand no one is reinventing any wheels; they're just continuing to improve so they can continue to grow market share or profits or both. If only there were no annoying managers in their way.

Replacement phrases: No replacement needed; embrace change and just stop saying this one.

See also: *If It Ain't Broke Don't Fix It*

30,000-Pound Gorilla

Once Quinlan hired Dvorak to ride shotgun at his meetings, the employees began paying attention.

Riding Shotgun

For the Millennials and younger reading this tome, *riding shotgun* did not originate from the late twentieth century practice of yelling "shotgun" when the vehicle in which you would be riding was in view.

Being the first to scream "shotgun" in these instances earned you the front passenger seat; and banished everyone other than the driver to the back.

Riding shotgun originally referred to the man who rode alongside the driver of a stagecoach or other horse-drawn transport. He was armed with pistols and a long gun – sometimes a shotgun – and his job was to protect the stagecoach and its contents from bandits and others – by lethal force, if necessary.

Today, when your annoying manager or coworker says he or she will be *riding shotgun* on this deal or in that meeting, they're not telling you they plan to shoot dead anyone who threatens you, they're just saying they will be there to assist.

Of course, this begs the question, why don't they just say "assist?"

Because they're annoying, that's why

Replacement phrases: Assist

See also: *Run Interference; Point Person*

30,000-Pound Gorilla

"The consultant told us that by calling it 'rightsizing' the laid-off employees are 32% less likely to sue us."

Rightsizing

This irritating, politically-correct term for "cutting expenses" vaulted into the vernacular during the 2007-2008 recession.

Because so many businesses were forced to make tough decisions, and those decisions most often included expense reductions and layoffs, annoying executives who cowardly felt uneasy using real-world terminology to describe their actions took the weakling's way out and declared they were *rightsizing* their organizations.

Of course, if it were truly *rightsizing*, they'd be doing it during good times too, wouldn't they? In fact, *rightsizing* would be a constant activity.

Rightsizing, by the way, is really a euphemism of a euphemism. Downsizing, the original euphemism for layoffs, morphed into *rightsizing* to make it easier for those not being rightsized right out of a job sleep better at night.

We hope they forever have nightmares.

Replacement phrases: Downsizing; Layoffs

See also: *Transition Phase*

30,000-Pound Gorilla

"A rising tide may lift all boats, but mine is still the biggest."

Rising Tide Lifts All Boats

This annoying analogy most often refers to the market forces affecting your industry. If the market is growing, everyone grows… even those companies with poor execution.

The inference is the underperformers in the industry might be growing their sales, but they're losing market share.

This phrase, like so many in this book, is mostly annoying in its overuse. However, like a few others, this one is made extra-annoying because it's unnecessary filler; worthless; wasted breath.

Once a manager latches onto this one, she'll never let it go. Suddenly, every situation is relatable to tides and their impact on boats.

Ugh; save us.

Additionally, and this is maddening, *rising tide lifts all boats* is sometimes used passive-aggressively by pompous managers to take a shot at someone or some team in their own organization.

The situation goes roughly like this: Your division delivered record results last month. However, instead of allowing you and your coworkers to bask in a little glory, some blockhead manager of another division (one that didn't fare as well) will dampen the festivities by reminding everyone that a *rising tide lifts all boats*.

Piss off, sore loser.

Replacement phrases: No replacement necessary; this one has never added anything to any conversation.

See also: *Raise the Bar*

30,000-Pound Gorilla

"Actually, he's lousy at just about everything; though, we keep him around because he's so good at running interference."

Run Interference

The precise meaning on this one is not always clear. Your annoying manager will tell you, "I need you to *run interference* for me on this one." Yet, what does that mean in this case?

The last time she said it, you were expected to be the *point person* on a project; though in an earlier instance, you were tasked with keeping the client in the dark. Of course – and this is the most annoying part – neither of those fits the literal definition of *run interference*, which is to protect someone from distractions or interruptions.

If this is what you're asking, then we are less annoyed. If you're looking for us to protect you from distractions, there really isn't a good replacement phrase in this case. However, if you just want us to keep someone in the dark, say that. If you want us to take charge of a project, say that.

However, if you just enjoy shoehorning *run interference* into everything we face day to day in the workplace, then please shut up.

Replacement phrases: No replacement needed when used correctly. In all other instances just say what you mean.

See also: *Point Person; Direct the Traffic*

30,000-Pound Gorilla

"I still don't understand why he has to run every new product up the flagpole."

Run it Up the Flagpole

You're an annoying manager and you want additional opinions on an idea, task, or project. Because you're an annoying manager, you cannot simply say, "Let's gather additional opinions on this one."

No, you're compelled to order that we *run it up the flagpole*.

This is why we all secretly hate you; you're making our heads hurt with your senseless jargon.

If there's one commonality among annoying managers, it's that they will never go for the direct when there's an idiom, cliché, analogy, or metaphor to be used. Why would they? *Run it up the flagpole* sounds so much cooler (in their minds) than "gather opinions" or "see what the team thinks."

Want to hear this one get really annoying? You may not have noticed, but we guarantee your annoying manager is often redundantly redundant with this one.

Think about it. We're sure you've heard some version of, "*Run it up the flagpole* to gather some additional opinions and see what the team thinks."

Ugh. We are going to be sick.

Replacement phrases: Gather opinions

See also: *Waterfall; Cascade*

30,000-Pound Gorilla

"Clearly, our best strategy is to encourage more pooch screwing."

Screw the Pooch

An earlier annoying phrase we examined, *rightsizing*, is what's known as a euphemism. That is, it's not just a replacement or synonym, but a nicer way to say something.

Screw the pooch is the exact opposite of a euphemism (unfortunately, there is no true antonym for euphemism, so let's just call this an unnecessary and odd vulgarity).

Screw the pooch refers to making a gigantic, perhaps career-ending mistake; that is, screwing up royally.

While a euphemism is used to soften the impact of a phrase, *screw the pooch* is used to overemphasize the issue at hand. We would argue unnecessarily; though, there are those who believe accusing someone of making a gigantic mistake is not enough; that it needs more "oomph," if you will.

To those managers we say this: are you really that comfortable discussing bestiality at work? Moreover, can making a mistake – regardless of how large – even compare?

Gross.

Replacement phrases: Gigantic mistake; Colossal error

See also: *Shit the Bed; Drop the Ball*

30,000-Pound Gorilla

"Apparently, we didn't get a seamless integration when we combined the accounting teams."

Seamless Integration

When you read the title of this one, you likely thought, "Hmm, why wouldn't we want *seamless integration*? Sounds beneficial."

You're correct. Everyone with a stake in an integration should want it to go seamlessly. The annoyance with this one occurs when *seamless integration* is used to describe the desired outcome of everything.

Seamless integration is one of those annoying phrases someone latches onto because it makes them (they believe) sound intelligent. Suddenly and forever, everything requires a *seamless integration*.

"We'll want to ensure there's a *seamless integration* with the new code we're adding to the software."

This usage is correct.

"Be sure we have a *seamless integration* with the new printers in the office."

This usage is borderline annoying.

"It's critical the relocated employees have a *seamless integration* into their new workspace."

This usage hurts our heads.

"Let's be certain we get a *seamless integration* with the caterer for tomorrow's meeting."

This usage makes us want to harm someone.

Replacement phrases: Perfect; Perfectly; Though, in the rare instance this is used correctly, there's no replacement phrase needed.

See also: *Synergistically; Sync*

30,000-Pound Gorilla

The team never forgot that time the shit literally hit the fan.

Shit Hits the Fan

Do you like using this one around the office? Do you think its use is kind of funny; maybe a little dangerous, but still kind of cute when you say it?

Okay, then picture it in your mind. You know… think about the exact moment when the *shit hits the fan*… literally… hits… the… fan.

Okay, yuck.

Shit hits the fan is annoying in its imagery and overuse; but, it's especially annoying when followed by that self-satisfying look (you know, the no-pun-intended-shit-eating-grin) the user cannot help but display after uttering it.

He'll warn you, "I think the shit's gonna hit the fan," and then his face tells you he thinks he's pretty freaking cool.

When the *shit hits the fan* is meant to describe the moment things go awry, unplanned, or especially become chaotic. If that's the case, why not just say that?

We'll tell you why. Because pretentious potty-mouths in your office love the attention this one gives them – ooh, he cussed; how cool of him. And, we'll argue, they love dramatic overemphasis.

They can't help it. They're annoying.

Replacement phrases: Problems; Chaos

See also: *Shit the Bed; Jump the Shark*

30,000-Pound Gorilla

"If no one admits who shit the bed, I'm docking everyone's pay."

Shit the Bed

If as an adult you ever *shit the bed*, it was likely a personal matter, correct? You didn't share this information with your coworkers, did you?

Okay, then we're confused how this one became so ubiquitous in many businesses today. Certainly, the increased open use of vulgar slang in the office holds a little blame; though, how in the world did *shit the bed* become a semi-acceptable way of describing the act of making a mistake?

Truly, how many people have ever literally *shit the bed*?

Of course, we don't really care and certainly don't want to know.

While this one is annoying on many levels, the clear winner of the annoyance sweepstakes on *shit the bed* goes to the overusers. Like most office slang that includes a curse word, *shit the bed* users find enjoyment in saying it. They likely experience a quick dopamine rush when they do; therefore, they say it again and again until they're hooked.

If you're a *shit the bed* user, you must stop; you're annoying the rest of us. We don't think you're funny or cute or avant-garde. We just think you're an irritating ass, and we'd like to help you get better.

Of course, just like someone who's literally shit the bed on multiple occasions, one of the first steps is wanting to quit.

Replacement phrases: Make a mistake

See also: *Drop the Ball; Screw the Pooch*

"Because people don't like to shit where they eat, we've reduced lunchroom loitering by 95% since we combined it with the bathroom."

Shit Where You Eat

We are often told animals are smarter than humans because they don't shit where they eat. That is, they don't screw up their food source by deficating in or around it. Apparently, this implies we humans are likely to poop in the fridge or pantry if not properly warned. Animals know instinctively not to do this.

Of course, if you've ever owned two dogs at the same time (as we have), you know sometimes one or both will literally eat shit. Given that we've never done that, we like to think, "Now who's smarter?"

The phrase *shit where you eat*, when used at your work, is meant to warn someone not to mess up a good thing (like employment) with a selfish act (like an office affair or theft of company property).

Of course, if that's the intention of the phrase, why don't annoying managers just say "don't jeopardize your job with that" instead of going for the inaccurate descriptive of don't *shit where you eat*?

One, because their arrogance won't allow them to ever speak clearly; and two, because they're too cool for school. They've got a bag full of slang and they intend to use everything in that bag… every freaking day.

These managers, in fact, have so many annoying go-to phrases it's hard to keep up. Everything they say starts to feel like fingernails on a chalkboard, as the team begins to shut them out.

Forgive the language, but their use of annoying phrases could mean (one might argue) they're shitting where you and the rest of your coworkers eat.

Replacement phrases: There's no universal replacement, just speak clearly.

See also: *Bio Break; Eat Your Own Dog Food*

30,000-Pound Gorilla

"Cool, but do you think you can make one that doesn't show the seams?"

Show the Seams

It seems some annoying managers are obsessed with seams.

In one breath they want you to *show the seams* and in the next they don't. Seems like they should make up their minds about these seams. Especially given the divisiveness of seams.

Half the readers are thinking, "When did seams become a bad thing?" While the other half thinks, "Who wants to see the seams?"

We're with you… all of you. Moreover, we're motivated to get annoying managers to simply stop talking about seams and to start talking about what they really want.

If you're prone to tell others to *show the seams* or to not *show the seams*, we (and everyone in your workplace) would like you to consider using words like "details" or "processes" or "parts" or "plans" or whatever it is you specifically want us to show or not to show.

If that's not possible – and it's probably not – perhaps you could just decide whether exposed seams are inherently bad or good. Like poorly designed seams, it seems we're split on the subject.

Replacement phrases: Details; Plans

See also: *Warts and All*

30,000-Pound Gorilla

"When the company tried to break down the silos, Meeks built a box fort."

Silos

Unless you work on a farm, at a grain co-op, or in missile defense, you don't have *silos* in your workplace.

Describing the various factions, teams, and departments in your office as *silos* was once a simple and convenient way to help organizations visualize how uncooperative various functions can be – and how to improve overall cooperation by "tearing down" the *silos*.

However, like similar helpful metaphors adapted in the workplace, the term *silos* has run its course… and now it's just mind-numbingly annoying when your HR director speaks about "breaking down the *silos* to achieve a cohesive blah, blah, blah."

Silos are, unfortunately, a favorite among the annoying human resources people at your work.

Oops, sorry about being redundant there; let's restate that. Silos are, unfortunately, a favorite among the human resources people at your work. (There, no redundancies in that sentence.)

Replacement phrases: Departments; Factions; Functions; Teams

See also: *Circular Firing Squad; Synergistically*

30,000-Pound Gorilla

Jim always won at poker night because he had more skin in the game.

Skin in the Game

In some ways, *skin in the game* is sometimes a little gross. Strike that; it's always a lot gross.

We, like many of you, either picture the annoying manager who blurted out this disturbing phrase lying naked, spread eagle, skin exposed on the conference room table.

Yuck.

Or, we picture the speaker's epidermis sloughing off and creating small piles of skin everywhere.

Double yuck.

Your annoying manager loves to talk about having *skin in the game*. His or her intention is to explain someone has something to lose. That person or department is invested in the results.

Additionally, when mentioning they're own *skin in the game*, the phrase often becomes an unnecessarily pompous way to demonstrate to you that they believe they're the only ones who really care about some outcome. It's often braggadocio disguised as concern with a little bit of "why don't the rest of you start pulling your weight" thrown in.

It's passive-aggressive and it makes our ears bleed.

Worse, it's often uttered by those who aren't truly invested in a company or project. Their money is not on the line; their jobs are not in jeopardy. They're just weak managers trying to sound strong.

If this describes you, instead of telling us you have *skin in the game*, why don't you try taking some personal responsibility and help the rest of the organization succeed?

Novel concept for annoying managers, isn't it?

Replacement phrases: Equity; Something to lose; Invested

See also: *Dog in this Fight; Ownership*

30,000-Pound Gorilla

"Unfortunately, I had a cold when I hired Aguirre; so, I couldn't conduct a proper smell test."

Smell Test

We have a belief that if something needs a *smell test*, assume the worst and just move on.

For example, if the date on the milk shows last week, just move on. No *smell test* needed. Similarly, if you think what you stepped in might be dog poop, assume the worst and move on.

The outcome of even a negative *smell test* in these instances makes us gag.

Somehow, the annoying managers at your work decided to utilize a *smell test* to evaluate everything.

"Does it pass the *smell test?*" they'll ask when speaking about a proposal from a vendor.

"He didn't pass the *smell test*," they'll tell you when referring to a candidate they didn't hire.

"Please give it a *smell test*," they'll ask when you're headed off to try a new restaurant for lunch.

Ugh, so annoying.

If only we could get them to stop.

The next time an annoying manager asks you about the results of a *smell test*, just lean in and take a loud, long sniff of him. Then look him in the eye and say without emotion, "I'll let you know."

While this likely won't end this manager's use of *smell test*, it will probably mark the last time you'll be around to hear it.

Replacement phrases: The replacement for this one is whatever metric you're trying to gauge. For example, "Do you think he'll make a good salesperson?"

See also: *Pass Muster*

The company decided to end the "so" drinking game after the first hour.

So

To be clear, *so* has a necessary place in the English language. When your meaning is "thus" or "accordingly," or when speaking about extremes, *so* can be a good choice. However, those uses are not what can make this one *so, so* annoying.

Most often uttered by young CEOs of hotshot startups and the exceedingly pompous, *so* has become *so* unnecessarily used and overused in business that it borders on maddening.

If you haven't been paying attention, the word *so* is getting added (for no discernable reason) to the beginning of sentences (especially when the pompous are answering a question). This makes the speaker sound like a 13-year-old girl explaining her frustration with the latest drama rocking the world of the eighth-grade elite.

This practice has become *so* ubiquitous on channels like CNBC (where they tend to interview a lot of Millennial CEOs), we've considered creating a drinking game. Every time someone on television starts a sentence with *so*, the audience must drink a shot.

In our informal testing, Steve lasted eight minutes.

"*So*, we just released our latest…" "*So*, we are considering moving into the…" "*So*, that's certainly something we're considering."

So annoying.

Are you nervous; are you confused; or, as we suspect, are you *so* in love with your own voice and opinion you believe every sentence needs an introduction?

So, that's what we were thinking, anyway.

So, when can you use so to start a sentence? Here's our rule: If you can't replace *so* with therefore or very, you're using it *so, so* annoyingly.

So, stop it.

Replacement phrases: No replacement; just stop adding it to the beginning of every response.

See also: *That Said*

30,000-Pound Gorilla

"We want to thank today's solutions provider, Madame Verdugo, for allowing us to incorporate her love potion in our latest consumer offering."

Solutions Provider

This irritating phrase is the combination of two unnecessarily verbose words. Neither solutions nor provider is required when we're just talking about a vendor or a supplier.

Plus, almost no company really buys all that many solutions… they buy stuff. They may think they're "sourcing the best *solutions provider*" for a specific need, but they're really just buying things… without any thought given to an actual solution.

In the past, you were asked to find a good price on copy paper. Today, annoying managers want you to discover a superior office products *solutions provider*.

Where you once purchased a new phone system; today, you must contract a communications *solutions provider*.

A couple of decades ago, your company may have used an ad agency, and the person in your role was tasked with managing their invoices. Today, your boss wants you take *ownership* of the marketing *solutions provider*.

Ugh… such a waste of words… so unnecessary… and so very annoying.

The good news is there's a bit of a reprieve we get with this one. If you pay attention, you'll notice managers will call these companies *solutions providers* when you're asked to hire them, and vendors when you're asked to fire them.

That's a tiny win… we suppose.

Replacement phrases: Vendor; Supplier

See also: *Client Engagement*

When the team decided to focus on everything from soup to nuts, they left out some important product lines.

Soup to Nuts

One of the many issues with *soup to nuts* is that it often follows the words "everything from" as in "this includes everything from *soup to nuts*."

Of course, the word "everything" already indicates this includes… well… everything. Adding *soup to nuts* after "everything from" becomes annoyingly redundant.

Another major irritant with this phrase is its age.

Anyone using *soup to nuts* in your office today should be banished… to a retirement home. With origins in the nineteenth century (that's the 1800s for the ordinally-challenged among you), *soup to nuts* should've run its course decades ago.

Unfortunately, it did not.

While the original meaning of *soup to nuts* was basically "beginning to end" (in reference to a typical multi-course dinner in the 1800s, which might begin with a bowl of soup and end with a serving of nuts), it's now simply used in business to describe "everything."

Given the typical multi-course dinner today begins with a Big Mac and ends with one of those ever-shrinking, though always lava-hot centered Baked Apple Pies, we think we can all agree *soup to nuts* sounds… well… nuts.

Certainly, it would be great if we could ignore those still holding a spot for *soup to nuts* in their vocabulary, but that's not always possible or practical. In lieu of ignoring them, we recommend always replying, "Twenty-three skidoo," when an annoying manager utters this antique phrase.

Replacement phrases: Everything

See also: *Warts and All*

30,000-Pound Gorilla

"I had no idea where I would work in the IT space; but I'm glad I ended up in the space space."

Space

At every company there's at least one annoying manager who's co-opted the perfectly harmless word *space* and morphed it into ear-bleeding terms like "ecommerce *space*," "IT *space*," "wholesale *space*," or "sales *space*" – just to name a few.

Are these pests referencing an entire industry or just a function within an industry? Are they speaking about a market, a department, or a specialty? Who knows?

Our guess is not even that annoying guy referring to everything as some sort of *space* knows.

Do you have one of these *space* guys in your office and wonder how he was created? It's simple, really. He heard *space* misused in this manner a couple of times; he liked how using *space* this way made the speaker sound savvy; then suddenly everything he referenced began to fit neatly into some *space*.

We fear this misuse of *space* will never go away, so we are proposing we make it ubiquitous. That is, the rest of us should start referring to everything in this manner.

Work in a pet store? Ask a coworker what they think the future is for the kitten *space*.

Manage a 7-11? Brag about your prowess in the candy bar *space*.

Sitting in a bar? Ask the bartender what first attracted him to the alcohol *space*.

At the gym? Inquire at the front desk how the staff feels about the sweaty towel *space*.

Absurd? Yes. Fun? Yes.

Will it stop the annoying guy in your office from referring to everything as a *space*? Unfortunately, there appears to be no hope of that.

Replacement phrases: No replacement needed if you're referring to a function (like sales). Otherwise, Industry or Market.

See also: *Of the World, The (Blanks)*

30,000-Pound Gorilla

"My bad. When he told me he was an expert at spinning the plates, I thought he meant he could multitask."

Spinning the Plates

In the last century, plate spinners delivered a pretty cool show. Television viewers (back when we only had three channels) were glued to their sets while Johnny (Carson) or Mike (Douglas) or Ed (Sullivan) watched in awe as a competent plate spinner kept a dozen or more plates spinning, suspended on long sticks.

The television viewing public, of course, had few choices then, so it took little to keep us entertained. Today, when your annoying manager mentions his prowess at *spinning the plates*, he's referring to multitasking.

He'll tell you how he's busy *spinning the plates*, while he's really just jerking off. (Not literally, you of the dirty mind… figuratively.)

Anyone who claims their job is like *spinning the plates* or *herding cats* is just a weak-minded soul who craves attention (and pity) more than he wants to truly help the business grow.

Give him the pity he desires… that is, pity how pathetic and annoying he is in delivering any semblance of leadership to you and the rest of the team.

And remember, *spinning the plates* never accomplished anything in the end. It was fun to watch… at time when there was nothing else to do.

Replacement phrases: No replacement needed… just do your job and stop telling everyone how hard it is.

See also: *Herding Cats; Trying to Boil the Ocean*

30,000-Pound Gorilla

"Oh, you can put your stake in the ground here... but you'll pay for it."

Stake in the Ground

In any office, announcing you are putting a *stake in the ground* has always been annoying on the surface; though today it's especially annoying because it seems to have multiple – often nonsensical – meanings.

Used correctly, *stake in the ground* should be akin to making a claim. For example, in the late 1800s, those involved in a land rush could claim acreage for themselves or their clan by being the first to put their *stake in the ground* – staking a claim to that land. Not important to this discussion, but when they gave up their claim, they were said to be pulling up stakes.

Makes sense, right?

Okay, now let's examine how your annoying manager misuses this phrase. We've heard *stake in the ground* uttered to imply drawing a *line in the sand*. We've heard it used to mark the beginning of a project. We've heard it said to reference an investment.

Rarely do we hear *stake in the ground* used to imply a do-nothing boss is laying a claim to something. While that would still be annoying, at least it would be correctly annoying.

Replacement phrases: Given the multiple misuses of this phrase, there are too many possible replacements to list; just say what you mean.

See also: *Line in the Sand*

30,000-Pound Gorilla

"We finally solved the 'Great Office Refrigerator Crisis' by telling everyone to stay in their lanes."

Stay in Your Lane

Stay in your lane is unique among the annoying phrases in this book because – like *nothing burger* – it's relatively brand new to the lexicon of the douchey managers.

When used to humorously throw shade on a coworker by telling him, "*Stay in your lane*, Richardson;" this one is fine – even in its overuse. However, when uttered to keep someone in their place – or, at least the place your annoying manager believes someone belongs – it's not only irritating to the ears, it's genuinely cruel.

There's no excuse for a manager who slams an employee for trying to do more. While it's necessary in some jobs to keep everyone on track and focused on only their own role (for example, at SpaceX during a launch or at a hospital during a brain surgery), telling someone, "*stay in your lane*" should never be the way to accomplish this.

Of course, since most of us don't work at SpaceX or assist in delicate operations, there's almost never a good business reason for containing an employee's desires to do more. It breaks their spirit; and it leaves the company with either an underproductive, unmotivated worker-bee or an empty seat.

You see, great people won't stand for being told to do less – and, they won't work for assholes.

If you're among the annoying managers trying to keep others in their place, how about you *stay in your lane* and stick to playing online poker or surfing for porn on your laptop? This way, you can leave the real work to the rest of us.

Replacement phrases: No replacement needed; just stop trying to be so cool, hip, now, and wow with your innate cruelty.

See also: *Heavy Lifting; Nothing Burger*

30,000-Pound Gorilla

"It's taken me months, but I finally got the team to sync with each other."

Sync

Why do we suddenly need to *sync* with everyone? Notice we didn't write "get in *sync*," no, that would make too much sense – and it would be the correct way to use *sync* in these instances.

If you're like Steve, you've heard your share of annoying bosses urging you to "be sure to *sync* with Larry on that project."

I'm sorry; do what with Larry? No offense, but I don't bat for that team. (Not that there's anything wrong with that.)

Why is it *sync*, anyway? Why not merge or blend or fuse or meld?

Also – and this is part of what makes the use of *sync* so annoying in the office – that irritating manager asking you to *sync* with someone most often just wants you to meet with them and gain an understanding about whatever it is they're working on.

No need to *sync* with Larry, just have him *level set* you so you're *up to speed* and you're both *on the same page*.

Ugh… maybe *sync* is not so bad after all.

Replacement phrases: Get in sync; Come to an agreement; Become fully informed

See also: *On the Same Page; Level Set; Up to Speed*

"At first I was concerned about her multiple personality disorder, but since they work synergistically, she maintains the highest productivity in the company."

Synergistically

Truly, this one should've never made the cut.

Synergistically is the adverbial form of synergistic, which basically means "working together in a productive manner." *Synergistically* describes how the team worked or should work; as in, "they did so *synergistically*."

Beautiful! Exactly what we need from our teams!

Therefore, *synergistically* should be okay to use in the office, right? Not so fast.

While generally used correctly in the workplace, *synergistically* is included in our list because like many annoying words and phrases your boss sometimes uses correctly, he or she feels *synergistically* must now be applied to everything.

Everything must be in harmony; every detail must *sync* with every other detail; everyone must work together on everything. There's no longer any room for individual action or initiative – regardless of how effective – we need the team working *synergistically* to solve everything… All. The. Time.

Got a big project coming up? Let's be sure to work *synergistically* with accounting.

Looking to rebrand an outdated offering? Great, we believe Frasier can help you *synergistically sync* with the marketing team.

Is the breakroom fridge loaded with expired condiments and more than a few poorly-covered mystery dishes? Terrific, be sure to work with the other department heads so you can *synergistically* create a long-term solution.

Ugh… truly awful.

Replacement phrases: No replacement needed… just slow down a bit, partner. Not everything or everyone needs to work *synergistically*.

See also: *Sync*

30,000-Pound Gorilla

"Do you think we can take this battle offline?"

Take it Offline

"Can we take it *offline*?" is sometimes a legitimate request, though mostly it's used as a weak way to brush off a pesky subordinate trying just a bit too hard.

You hear this one when annoying managers request certain discussions be curtailed until a more appropriate time by asking the speaker, "Can we take if *offline*?"

What they're really saying is simply, "What you want to discuss is not important to me, so I'm going to ask you to shut the hell up for the rest of the meeting."

When you hear it, you know your miserable, self-important boss wants you and your coworkers to discuss your idea amongst yourselves… on your time. Of course, you're thinking, "Well, lah-dee-dah! He's too busy, too important, or too stupid to hear my ideas? I suppose I'll spend the rest of the day searching online for a new gig or simply surfing horrendous websites on my company computer. What I'm not going to do is anything productive."

This one's annoying because it's insulting, overused by jerk bosses, and it's unnecessarily passive-aggressive. It's a weak move.

We'd all have more respect for the manager if he just told us the truth. Of course, if you want to hear the truth in your office, you'll probably have to *take it offline*.

Replacement phrases: No replacement needed, just start telling the truth. After all, we're told it will set you free.

See also: *Put it on the Back Burner; Put a Pin in It*

30,000-Pound Gorilla

Due to his depth perception, Vogelheim's notches were always just a bit off.

Take it Up/Down a Notch

If we were talking about speedometers or a volume control, *take it up/down a notch* works beautifully. It describes the exact amount in which the situation needs to be moved up or down.

In business, the phrase has no actual nominal value and therefore can only be used as a lame, hollow attempt at motivation by your annoying (and ineffective) manager.

If your marketing budget is a bit bloated, your manager may have you *take it down a notch*.

What does that mean? What if your notches are closer together than hers? Suddenly, the fate of your company's success rides on your ability to interpret how many marketing dollars one notch represents? Yikes!

And here's a little tip: there's no Google conversion for notches to dollars. (We know; we checked.)

Especially when used as a pep talk, *take it up a notch* is vague. Moreover, it's the kind of weak leadership that do-nothing, rah-rah managers love to spew.

Of course, if your manager wants you to *take it up a notch*, he or she isn't asking for all that much.

Think about it. How much is a notch? It's one decibel (sound), one mile per hour (speed), or one rung (on a ladder). Despite how maddening the request is, we're pretty sure you won't break a sweat complying.

Replacement phrases: No replacement needed; just do the math. Replace this saying with the number you want to add or cut from something. And if what you're dealing with isn't numerical, just strike the phrase entirely.

See also: *Next Level*

30,000-Pound Gorilla

"The rest of you could learn a thing or two from Mr. Maes about being a team player."

Team Player

We'll admit it; we like referring to a group of employees as a team. In so many ways and in so many workplaces, successful groups of employees act like well-coached teams.

However, we must draw the line at calling anyone a *team player*.

If they're loyal, call them loyal. If they're dedicated, call them dedicated. If they're willing to help you cover up malfeasance, they're not a *team player*, they're an accessory to a crime.

Of course, most often when your annoying manager refers to someone as a *team player*, they're indicating the person is loyal and/or dedicated. Your boss utters the overused and irritating phrase *team player* because he or she is of the fauxtivational type who sprinkles in sports analogies, sayings, and metaphors with excruciating frequency.

Barely a sentence leaves their mouth that doesn't include such cringe-worthy gems as *play ball*, *game time*, *move the goal posts*, and of course, *team player*.

While all managers want employees to be loyal and dedicated, annoying managers don't understand employee loyalty and dedication are tested with every irritating cliché they utter.

Replacement phrases: Loyal; Dedicated

See also: *Play Ball; There is No "I" in Team*

30,000-Pound Gorilla

"I want to thank Reuther for providing such a complete tear down of our main competitor."

Tear Down, The

The basic definition of "tear down" should be clear to all; that is, to dismantle, disassemble, or even destroy something or someone. If this was the only way your annoying manager used these words, they wouldn't be included here.

Today, managers and executives are requesting information in a most irritating way: they're asking you to provide *the tear down*.

"Poremba, be sure and give me *the tear down* on that one."

"We're going to need to see *the tear down* before we move forward, Mike."

Excruciating.

If hearing someone ask for *the tear down* doesn't make you want to tear down the cubicle walls in the entire office, then you're not paying attention.

Of course, it's more than the misuse of the words that makes this one annoying; it's the pretentiousness in the delivery that causes you to grit your teeth so hard you'll give yourself a migraine.

Relax.

Don't let the annoying workplace hordes win. Instead, fight back in the name of sanity and clarity.

When asked to provide *the tear down*, turn your head as if confused and simply reply, "*The tear down?*" Then stare at your annoying boss until she provides a clarifying word or phrase. Don't let the uncomfortable silence affect you. Hold your stare, keep your blinking to a minimum, and shut up.

Do this every time you're asked for *the tear down*, and she'll likely get the message after no more than six or seven thousand utterances. (No one said any of this was going to be easy.)

Replacement phrases: Analysis; Inspection

See also: *Do a Deep Dive*

30,000-Pound Gorilla

"If the board asks about the quarterly report, just tell them I'm teeing it up."

Tee it Up

If your boss is a scratch golfer (basically someone who spends too much time golfing and not enough time leading), he'll often ask you to *tee it up*.

Oh cool, we see what you did there. You used a golfing term as a metaphor instead of simply asking us to prepare or present something. Aren't you the fancy one?

Workplace golfers – and especially managers and executives who golf – are annoying even if they never spoke a single phrase listed in this book. Think about it. They're excessively tan year-round; their faces are often dotted with dry, scaly patches; and their calves resemble oversized cantaloupes.

Of course, they're especially annoying because they cannot shut up about golf.

Every Monday you get a shot-for-shot replay of the 36 holes they played over the weekend.

Every Tuesday you hear about their planned Wednesday outing and a shot-by-shot recap of the last time they played that course.

Thursdays are filled with memories of Wednesday (again, shot-by-freaking-shot).

And while Fridays bring more golf talk, your annoying golfer-boss spares you by leaving early "to hit a bucket" of range balls before his big weekend of golf.

Ugh.

This existence would be bad enough if it stopped there; but, of course, it does not. He (yes, it's almost always a he in these cases) asks you constantly to *tee it up*.

Time to start the meeting? *Tee it up*.

Need to prepare for a client visit? *Tee it up*.

Got a question? *Tee it up*.

When he want the TV in the breakroom tuned to the Golf Channel… *tee it up*.

Golfers are the worst managers.

Replacement phrases: Plan; Prepare; Present

See also: *Par for the Course*

After the disaster of the 'so' drinking game, the office's 'that said' version was an even worse idea during Patterson's presentation.

That Said

Merely unnecessary filler, *that said* can and should be stricken from the vocabulary of every English-speaking man, woman, and child. If it was, we'd lose nothing, as this saying is worthlessly annoying.

It provides no value and adds nothing to any conversation.

That said, we were curious if other languages were similarly plagued with this annoying two-word combination.

That said, we did some digging.

That said, unfortunately for workers everywhere, *that said* does not discriminate.

While enojoso (annoying) managers in Mexico City are routinely beginning sentences with *dicho esto*, their Russian counterparts are uttering *shto skazal* before they too make their delo (case).

That said, if nothing else, the universal annoyance with *that said* might be the unifying factor that simultaneously solves America's immigration and collusion/election interference issues.

That said, we're not holding our breath.

Replacement phrases: Therefore. Though, generally speaking, there's no replacement needed, as this one is most often unnecessary filler.

See also: *At the End of the Day; So*

"Sorry Vetter; but saying 'there's a first time for everything' does not adequately explain our impending bankruptcy."

There's a First Time for Everything

No shit? *There's a first time for everything?* Well thank you Captain Obvious!

Can we all just agree right now *there's a first time for everything?* And, since we all agree, would it be possible for the annoying fools in your office to drop this one from their vocabulary?

That's unlikely.

Just because *there's a first time for everything* doesn't mean you're a genius for pointing this out… multiple times a week… in the most annoying manner possible.

This phrase is annoying because of how and why it's used. It's never used to share knowledge – it's almost always said sarcastically. It's never uttered as a compliment – it's nearly always used to diminish an accomplishment.

Byerly just made salesperson of the month? Well, *there's a first time for everything.*

Kraig showed up on time today? Well, *there's a first time for everything.*

Shelby passed his certification? Well, *there's a first time for everything.*

You know what we and the rest of your coworkers want to experience as a first? We'd love for you to go a whole day without uttering your annoying, snarky clichés and other dried-up jargon.

We'd love to experience eight business hours without cringing or having our ears bleed.

We know *there's a first time for everything…* we're just waiting for the first time we can be at work for an entire day without hearing an annoying phrase fall from your lips.

Replacement phrases: No replacement needed; just stop being an ass.

See also: *Easier Said Than Done; Are Two Different Things; It Is What It Is*

30,000-Pound Gorilla

Buchanan fired Iris and Ian because he lived by the saying 'there is no I in team'.

There is No "I" in Team

Common, clichéd phrases like *there is no "I" in team* are simply painful to hear. Most of the jargon in this book is harmless to a group's progress, and merely just irritating.

There is no "I" in team is different.

If just used to motivate the group, it would be acceptably annoying. Unfortunately, *there is no "I" in team* is almost never used to improve true team dynamics. Instead, it's most often voiced as a way to crush individualism and personal initiative, while driving for lockstep consensus.

The annoying managers who spout *there is no "I" in team* are not simply annoying, they're dangerous.

They're pushing for groupthink in organizations that desperately need creativity.

These managers are like the Kumbaya crowd – those who push for open offices and uniformity among all layers of the company. Nice thought; but while these concepts might work at Google, experience shows they don't work in the real world.

If everyone always did what was best for the company, we never would've invented managers.

Unfortunately, when we invented managers, we got all types. We got some great leaders and we got some jerks whose push for consistency is killing your team's ability to innovate.

While *there is no "I" in team*, there is an M and an E; and if you're not going to let me be me, then why did you hire me in the first place?

Replacement phrases: No replacement needed – unless, of course, you want to replace the manager who can't stop saying this idiotic phrase.

See also: *Team Player*

30,000-Pound Gorilla

That moment the team realized Niall didn't think like everyone else in the office.

Think Outside the Box

Likely the most infamous of annoying manager phrases, *think outside the box* has gone from brilliance to cliché in less than a generation.

While this saying once forced us to cleverly consider how we attack problems; today, it merely forces us to hold back a light chuckle or a small puke.

More than any other annoying phrase in your manager's arsenal, *think outside the box* signifies your manager is worthy of your contempt. By telling you unironically to *think outside the box*, your manager is telling you that he or she is not an adult, but a dolt. Someone so vapid and unoriginal they're likely to bankrupt the company just by showing up.

If this describes your manager, you have a choice: quit now or be further sucked into the void.

Of course, some of you think working for a manager this dense is a good thing. You believe he or she is bound to get fired when the big boss learns just how truly simpleminded he or she is, right?

Wrong! The big boss either hired and/or promoted this dimwit. The big boss is likely a dimwit too. Moreover, when a dimwit becomes a manager, they never leave. Ever.

Time to dust off the resume and *think outside the box*.

Replacement phrases: Think creatively; Look at the problem differently; Try something new

See also: *Paradigm Shift*

"Ever since Paglia started calling himself a thought leader, he spends most of the day staring at the ceiling."

Thought Leader

You may want to argue that *thought leader* is just an annoying imaginary title and not an annoying phrase. You'd be wrong.

While *thought leader* is certainly one of the most annoying made-up titles that gets thrown around nearly every industry, it's beginning to creep into the vernacular of the self-anointed *thought leaders* you work with.

To be clear, self-anointed are the only kind of *thought leaders* we encounter today. To add some credence to their overblown opinion of themselves, you'll find these annoying *thought leaders* anointing others.

"Yes, that Romig is a real *thought leader*."

No he's not; Romig just talks a lot… as do you.

The odd concept of *thought leader* in most industries today is based on prolificity and not production.

That is, those who have an opinion about everything; who fill their social media timelines with clichéd memes; who pontificate at every turn about all subjects – in other words, who never seem to shut up – think of themselves as *thought leaders*.

They are not. They are talk leaders. Annoying talk leaders, to be sure.

Replacement phrases: No replacement needed.

See also: *Guru*

30,000-Pound Gorilla

"Explain to me again how calling your department's catastrophic loss the 'total-total' makes the numbers look better?"

Total-Total

Total-total is to *net-net* what a solar eclipse is to a light bulb.

Hearing an annoying manager use *total-total* the first time feels like a rare, almost holy experience. It's spoken with such confidence – and it just rolls off the tongue – like it's really a thing.

After a few seconds basking in the faint echo of *total-total*, you realize it's not a thing. There is no *total-total*… but, that doesn't matter, you think, it was still a cool thing for your manager to say.

You feel this way until he says it a second time; in a different meeting. Now, you start thinking he's a little slow. You forgive him these two indiscretions until you hear him go all-in on this abomination and utter it more than a dozen times in the same meeting.

In Steve's entire career, he's heard *total-total* used by just three managers. Of course, it felt like each of these three said it more than 100,000 times, *total-total*.

While annoying, there is still something magical about the use of *total-total* that we can't put our fingers on. It makes us smile when we hear it. It makes us smile the same smile we might display when a baby or a kitten does something worthy of sharing on social media.

Perhaps it's the playful innocence of the annoying speaker – like the playful innocence of a kitten.

Perhaps it's the childlike way he or she approaches the job.

Perhaps we're just smiling because it reveals how stupid this person in charge of us really is.

Yeah, it's that third thing.

Replacement phrases: Total; Net

See also: *Net-Net*

"... and Number 4: It's no longer appropriate to touch base with colleagues without first asking their permission."

Touch Base

Usually an annoyance uttered by a cold-calling salesperson, *touch base* is a soft (and maddening) way to request an unnecessary contact.

You've likely received the typical unwanted voicemail or email: "It's Joey over at The Lewis Company and I just wanted to *touch base* with you on our new widget." In other words, this salesperson wants to chew up your time to demo their worthless product or service via what feels like an innocuous attempt to *touch base*.

It's not innocuous; it's a timewaster of the highest order… run!

If Joey was confident in his offering, he'd ask for a firm meeting. Because he's not, he settles for some base-touching.

Keep your fingers on your own base, Joey.

When your annoying manager uses *touch base*, it's to signify a similarly unnecessary contact; though, with a cover-his/her-ass connotation added in: "Be sure to *touch base* with Grace on the new contract."

Translation: "I'm too weak to approve or deny whatever it is we're talking about, so I want you and another underpaid coworker to make the final decision. This way, I can keep my job if everything implodes."

No worries; we'll *touch base* all right. We'll *touch base* to compare notes about our weak manager.

Replacement phrases: Contact; Speak

See also: *Connect With; Reaching Out*

"That's Hartline. He's been in a transition phase for about six months."

Transition Phase

When your annoying boss uses the words *transition phase* to describe anything, there's a 99% chance something in your business is going very badly, no one knows exactly why, and there's no definitive plan to fix it.

Transition phase has become a rationalization by ineffective managers to explain the limbo period between yesterday's dumpster fire and tomorrow's disaster. It's the period of nothingness where everyone gets a free pass (think of it as your company's version of *The Purge* – only this one lasts a lot longer than 24 hours).

Transition phase can also be used as an excuse – a smokescreen, if you will – to explain away bad results.

Whatever the reason, no one wants to hear *transition phase* come from the mouths of anyone with authority at their workplace. It never means sales are growing; it never means profit is improving; it never means you're about to get a promotion.

In other words, it's never good news. Dust off your resume.

Replacement phrases: No replacement needed – instead, have a plan.

See also: *Rightsizing*

30,000-Pound Gorilla

"You won't be able to see her today because according to the new triage rules, you're no longer a priority."

Triage

Triage is a medical term that describes the process of determining the order of treatment when faced with a large number of patients. It takes place, for example, following a disaster where medical personnel are dealing with multiple injuries – each with its own degree of urgency.

Without proper *triage*, someone with a simple broken bone might receive care before someone missing a limb.

Proper *triage* is critical when lives are in the balance. Given that lives are not in the balance in your office, there's no reason your annoying manager should ask you to *triage* anything. Yet he does. All the time.

We've heard managers use *triage* to describe everything from assessing employees in a new acquisition to ranking the color swatches for the new lunchroom chairs.

Whatever the use in business, it's annoying… and it's incorrect. *Triage* is annoying in its misuse and overuse, but it's especially annoying because it's most often hyperbolic.

Hyperbole has no place in any workspace. Of course, when simply providing calm, collected thoughts about a topic is possible, your annoying manager reaches for unnecessary exaggeration.

Annoying managers love the drama when they're the ones creating it. Why describe something as it is when you can describe it in extreme terms? Why ask someone to review a document, plan for a meeting, or assess a competitive threat when you can insist they *triage* the situation?

Because you're annoying, that's why.

Replacement phrases: Assess; Plan; Review

See also: *Unpack*

30,000-Pound Gorilla

The new manager had the team concerned; and not just because he kept referring to everyone as his troops.

Troops

While the irritating, PC-driven evolution of employees becoming known as associates, tribe, teammates, crew members, etc. is certainly cause for cringe-worthy moments in the workplace, the use of *troops* to describe this bunch is downright maddening.

Troops, of course, refers to members of a troop – as in military troop, Girl Scout troop, etc.

Your company, division, department, or office is not a troop; it's a company, division, department, or office. You don't have *troops*, you have employees.

Now, while *troops* can also refer to a large number of something (for example, *troops* of onlookers crowded the sidewalk), this is not what your annoying manager means when he or she utters *troops*.

Most often heard by the bothersome Baby Boomers in charge, *troops* comes across as lockstep military with a glossy coating of faux motivation. It, like your boss, is old, tired, and transparently annoying.

Whether patriotic or idiotic, there's no reason in this millennium to refer to those selling to your customers, shuffling papers, or programming code as *troops*.

We have an idea. Let's all do our patriotic best and agree to support the *troops* – the real ones – and do so by not referring to our employees as *troops*… 'kay?

Replacement phrases: Employees; Team

See also: *Boots on the Ground*

30,000-Pound Gorilla

Unfortunately, Roger's first experiment to prove you couldn't boil the ocean was his last.

Trying to Boil the Ocean

Have you ever heard anything so stupid in your entire life?

Trying to boil the ocean is akin to trying to put the sun in a paper bag or trying to shrink Kim Kardashian's butt. It's not only not possible, it's just not right.

This begs the question: Why do annoying managers accuse others of *trying to boil the ocean*?

Because… umm… they're annoying? Because… they're likely the douchiest people you work with? Because… they want everything they say to sound insightful and cutting edge?

Because… all of the above?

Ding, ding, ding! We have a winner.

Your annoying, douchey manager wants to sound insightful and cutting edge; therefore, he constantly accuses others of *trying to boil the ocean* when they've done nothing more than suggest an alternative to the status quo.

God forbid we look at options. It'll be Armageddon if the team considers an alternate route. There will certainly be cats and dogs living together – mass hysteria, in other words – if we consider someone else's ideas.

Ugh. So annoying; so weak; so passive-aggressive.

Replacement phrases: No replacement necessary; just accept change and challenges to the status quo. It's called growing.

See also: *Herding Cats; Reinvent the Wheel*

30,000-Pound Gorilla

While Mitch never took the blame he deserved, at least his subordinates were warned.

Under the Bus

Apparently in thousands of workplaces across America, employees are being unjustly sacrificed for a variety of reasons. Whether it's to avoid blame themselves or to simply redirect the ire of their own superiors, the weak among the (mostly) manager class is busy throwing their subordinates *under the bus*.

If that's all they were doing, we'd just chalk it up to typical management. Unfortunately, they (and, of course, those being thrown) cannot stop talking about this imaginary bus and how they threw someone (or were thrown) under it.

If only they could shut up about it, right?

Of all the annoying jargon heard in the workplace, *under the bus* is among the worst.

When the thrower says it, it's self-congratulatory braggadocio.

When the throwee says it, it's self-pity in search of commiseration.

And the visual is always disturbing.

Of course, those who complain most often about being thrown *under the bus* are usually the underperformers on the team. Those, you might argue, deserving of being tossed in front of a moving bus.

Figuratively speaking, of course. ;)

Replacement phrases: Scapegoat; Sacrifice

See also: *Pass the Buck*

30,000-Pound Gorilla

"When I asked Harrington to unpack a couple of his ideas, I had no idea he'd take that as a sign to move in."

Unpack

You've just arrived at your hotel after a long flight. Likely, you want to simply *unpack* your luggage and chill. The act of unpacking in the real world is often a relaxing and almost always necessary activity.

Enter the self-proclaimed gurus from Human Resources. These annoying psycho-babblers hijacked a perfectly innocent word and made it mind-numbingly irritating.

Their use of *unpack* is never relaxing or necessary. It's typical, annoying HR-trying-to-be-PC-at-the-sake-of-sanity garbage. If only *unpack* never made it beyond these yutzes, right?

Once the HR crew started discussing the need to *unpack* our feelings or an issue, the rest of the annoying managers grabbed hold.

Now, we can't just have an idea, we need to *unpack* it. We can't just present a solution, we need to *unpack* it. It's gone beyond annoying... it's insanity.

The first sign you work for an idiot boss often begins with, "Let's *unpack* that," after you or a colleague suggest something that never needed any unpacking. Hearing this, you and the rest of the team immediately question your decision to ever join this company.

Everyone, you see, knows everything is downhill after that gem.

Replacement phrases: Discover; Investigate; Discuss

See also: *Triage*

30,000-Pound Gorilla

"I had to let him go. No matter what we asked him to do, he never could get up to speed on anything."

Up to Speed

You've just been added to an existing team working on an important project. Certainly, you need to quickly gain as much knowledge as possible if you hope to be an effective contributor. Your annoying manager, of course, explains to you and the group that you need to get *up to speed*.

How *up to speed* became synonymous with being fully informed we'll never know. We mean, we could look it up on Google, but we really don't care how this became a thing in the workplace. We just want it to stop.

Up to speed conjures up an image of the rest of the team running together; in one direction; away from the newbie. It seems even if the newbie got *up to speed*, they would still be behind the group, right?

This scenario just begs for an algebraic word problem.

For example, if the group is going 8 miles per hour, and the new member starts out 17 miles behind them at 4 miles per hour for the first two miles, then 8 miles per hour after that, how long would it take for the newbie to catch up?

The answer is, of course, infinity times a million! The newbie would never catch up if all he did was eventually get *up to speed*.

If your annoying manager refuses to say something like fully informed or up to date, perhaps we can get her to at least switch to *on the same page* or *sync*. Yes, these are also annoying, but certainly more aligned with the goal, right?

Replacement phrases: Fully informed; Up to date

See also: *On the Same Page; Level Set; Sync*

30,000-Pound Gorilla

"As you can see from this chart, Samek's overutilization of the lone stall in the men's room is harming the team's productivity."

Utilize/Utilization

These two words are perfectly fine when you mean *utilize* or *utilization*. These become annoying when you really mean use or use (as in "yooz" the verb or "yoos" the noun).

Utilize/utilization in place of use/use is overkill. Strike that. It's annoying overkill. Annoying managers *utilize* the word *utilization* to sound intelligent.

Of course, they do not… cannot… sound intelligent regardless of their word choice.

We sometimes like to call this government-employee-speak. No disrespect intended, but when you see police officers, the fire department's spokesperson, the mayor, or virtually any other government employee interviewed on television, they morph from an average human using everyday language into a robot programmed only to use the biggest words possible.

Instead of hearing about how the bad guy broke into the house using a screwdriver, we're subjected to, "The alleged perpetrator illegally entered the victim's residence penetrating the exterior ingress with the assistance of a flat, elongated, metal apparatus."

Clarity be damned in television interviews and, unfortunately, in your office.

Replacement phrases: Use

See also: *Hammer it Out; Impact*

30,000-Pound Gorilla

Surprisingly, Stringfellow closed more deals when he showed his clients his warts and all.

Warts and All

Okay, gross. We understand the warts, but what's the all?

Warts are bad enough, but somehow we're supposed to show the all, as well? Are they zits? Is it just dry skin? Could the all be something really disgusting like hemorrhoids, open sores, or even dingleberries?

Like we wrote: gross.

For whatever reason, your annoying manager feels the need to either reveal everything or nothing. Unfortunately, he or she indicates this by explaining either "We need to show him everything; *warts and all*," or, "There's no need to show the *warts and all*."

Forgive us, but we weren't planning to show any warts… and certainly not the all.

Instead of reaching for vague clichés, wouldn't it be grand if managers just provided guidance in specific, real terms? Imagine working for a company where direction was clear, and guidance was always provided in a timely, direct manner.

Just think how great it would be to work for someone who wielded the English language as it was intended to be used. Imagine going a whole day without hearing annoying jargon that causes your ears to bleed.

We can dream, can't we?

Replacement phrases: Everything

See also: *Show the Seams*

30,000-Pound Gorilla

"His ideas were so dumb, I decided to waterfall him instead of the ideas."

Waterfall

Sounds so peaceful, doesn't it? When you hear *waterfall*, your mind should take you to a beautiful forest setting where a crystal-clear stream flows freely over a small rock face.

Unfortunately – here in the real world – your annoying manager has co-opted this once scenic memory and turned it into an unrecognizable bastardization. Today's irritating bosses no longer want you to share information or gather opinions, they prefer you, "*Waterfall* that to the team."

Help us all!

Surviving in the workplace a half-century ago often meant laughing at your boss's dumb jokes.

We now affectionately call these "dad jokes" because the cringe-inducing punchlines are nothing compared to the sheer horror created by today's managers asking us to *waterfall* stuff to others. As bad as the boss's jokes were in the 1960s, we're pretty sure no one wanted to punch those knuckleheads in the mouth for sharing these.

Today, the best employees are those who can control their urge to scream and wildly throw fists into their manager's face when asked to *waterfall* something. These are the true workplace heroes.

#Heroes

Replacement phrases: Review

See also: *Run it Up the Flagpole; Cascade*

30,000-Pound Gorilla

"So, Mr. & Mrs. Johnson, tell me please, what keeps you up at night?"

What Keeps You Up at Night

When you run out of interesting things to say at business gatherings or good questions to ask a potential client, please do yourself a favor and shut up.

Asking, "*What keeps you up at night?*" will not endear you to the person; it will not make them respect you; and it will certainly not create thoughtful reflection in their brain. It will only make them cringe and want to get as far away from you as possible.

No one – and we do mean no one – truly shares this information with colleagues, coworkers, or potential vendors.

There are only two possibilities that come to mind when you ask someone this: (1) "Nothing keeps me up at night, and I think you're an idiot for asking such an asinine and contrived question;" or (2) "Something does keep me up at night, and you just made me think of it while looking at your face."

Instead of being intentionally annoying in these situations, try this: be yourself. Moreover, while it's good to prepare for most gatherings and meetings, make sure what you intend to speak about or ask doesn't make you look like a disingenuous jerk.

… Oh, and the answer is you. You and your contrived questions keep us up at night!

Replacement phrases: Most often, there's no replacement needed. However, if you really do care and you can genuinely provide assistance, try, "Do you face any challenges where you think I can help?"

See also: *Keep Me Looped-In*

30,000-Pound Gorilla

Everyone remembers the day the team tried to enter Gerardi's wheelhouse.

Wheelhouse

We've got bad news and great news about this one.

The bad news is that *wheelhouse* is another annoying business phrase borrowed from sports.

The great news is that it's the last annoying business phrase borrowed from sports included in this book!

If only this also marked the last time any of us would hear our hack of a manager discussing business using sports analogies, metaphors, and clichés.

Wheelhouse is a term annoying managers borrowed from baseball that baseball borrowed from industry. It originally referred to the housing or area around a wheel (like the paddle wheel on a steamboat).

At some point, baseball adopted *wheelhouse* to mean the area where a batter's swing is most effective – that is, where they would make the best contact with a pitch.

Today, annoying managers everywhere insist on equating competence at anything to one's *wheelhouse*.

Mosely's not very good at answering phones? Phones must not be in his *wheelhouse*.

Trudell's a pro at presenting to customers? Presentations must be in his *wheelhouse*.

Ugh.

Of course, if referring to competence or expertise as one's *wheelhouse* was the only use of this irritating jargon, we'd probably (try to) learn to live with it. It's never that simple with annoying bosses, is it?

If you really want your ears to bleed, think about the time Steve heard a manager use *wheelhouse* to describe (he believes) business acumen or intelligence. "Yeah, Frye really has the *wheelhouse* for that kind of thing?"

What. The. Heck?

What in the world does that even mean? We may never know because it's clearly outside our *wheelhouse*.

Replacement phrases: Expertise; Competence

See also: *Ballpark*

Ziegler's Bar was usually where the rubber met the road.

Where the Rubber Meets the Road

Everyone knows the rubber meets the road at the bottom of the tire. The tire is mounted on a wheel that's always spinning when your vehicle is in motion.

We suppose the idea here is that moving your vehicle matters most *where the rubber meets the road*. That is, it doesn't matter what the engine does unless it translates into a rotating tire connecting with the street in order to propel your vehicle forward.

Sometimes, this one is uttered as, "When the rubber meets the road" – which, of course, is something completely different.

Where the rubber meets the road is the point at which, in business, things become serious or perhaps finalized – depending entirely on how the annoying manager or executive using this cliché intended it.

That's a recurring problem with much of the overused jargon in this book: many phrases are so misused that the meaning is not always clear to the intended audience.

And, of course, that's *where the rubber meets the road* when it comes to any overused saying relayed by cliché-loving managers.

Replacement phrases: When it matters; Where it's important; The result

See also: *Mission Critical*

30,000-Pound Gorilla

"Nineteen innings! Are you sure you guys aren't going for a win-win scenario in this game?"

Win-Win Scenario

Allow us to overgeneralize a bit to introduce this phrase.

In a basic negotiation between two parties there are four possible outcomes: Party A can prevail against Party B; Party B can prevail against Party A; both Parties can fail; or both Parties can succeed.

That last example is called a *win-win scenario* – that is, everyone wins. Of course, this should be the desired outcome of all your negotiations; and it's even okay to say you're seeking a win-win outcome when walking into a negotiation.

The issue we have with this saying is the overuse and misuse by some managers. While many who use this term do so correctly (and sparingly), there is a portion of the management population that latched onto this phrase and will simply not let go.

They use *win-win scenario* for everything… all the time. In fact, they just won't shut up about *win-win scenarios*.

Any situation that can have multiple outcomes now becomes an example of something deserving of a *win-win scenario*. They see the proposed food order for a company lunch, and they utter, "Well, be sure we go for a *win-win scenario*."

They notice a new copier in the office and the first words out of their mouths are, "That's a real *win-win scenario*, isn't it?"

Of course, as bad as *win-win scenario* is, it pales in comparison to a win-win-win scenario or even a win-win-win-win scenario. Yes, we've heard as many as four wins uttered when an unimaginative manager was trying to impress a potential client.

If you haven't yet had the pleasure, believe us, it's as ear-bleeding as it sounds.

Replacement phrases: As with many misused terms, there are too many replacement phrases to list. Did your manager mean that both parties in a negotiation should win or was he really just trying to get everyone to compromise? (A comprise, by the way, is often the antithesis of a *win-win scenario*, as it's really a tie-tie scenario.)

See also: *Buy-In; On the Same Page*

30,000-Pound Gorilla

"I've decided to work smarter, not harder... and just have you do all the work."

Work Smarter, Not Harder

Why can't we do both?

Moreover, why are you assuming we're not working as smart as possible right now?

This saying is annoying primarily because your boss uses it when he believes you're an idiot. An idiot wasting time trying to complete a task the hard way.

"If only he was as smart as me," your boss thinks as he implores you to use your head and complete tasks more efficiently; more like he would do it.

Your boss is an ass; but then you already knew that, didn't you?

Like so many of the phrases in this book, this one doesn't really have a ready replacement because it never should have been said in the first place.

Work smarter, not harder is a placeholder for so many passive-aggressive ideas bottled up in your boss's little head we cannot begin to fathom what he should be using instead of this idiotic and obvious phrase.

He might mean "do your best" or he could be saying "you're doing it wrong, but I'm too much of a jerk to actually help you do it right, so I'm just going say something that makes me sound superior to you."

Either way, he's an ass.

Replacement phrases: No replacement needed; just please stop saying it.

See also: *Give 110%; Bring Your 'A' Game*

30,000-Pound Gorilla

"Does anyone other than Henderson need help wrapping their heads around the new project?"

Wrap (One's) Head Around

Physically impossible and impossibly annoying. This one is just hard to *wrap our heads around*.

To truly *wrap your head around* something would mean you were likely in a fatal car crash. And while we are assuming our annoying manager was referring to understanding something, we can never be so sure with this jerk.

The worst part about this irritating phrase is that it's most often used when discussing an uncomplicated matter. Additionally, it's sometimes a weak manager's way to tell you your idea sucks.

"Yeah… I just can't *wrap my head around* that one."

Translation: "I'm a small-minded jerk who doesn't want to listen to any ideas that did not hatch from my pea brain."

Regardless of the meaning, it's always annoying, nonetheless; and sadly, there are times a fatal car crash might feel like a better place to be than in another mind-numbing meeting with this annoying manager.

Replacement phrases: Understand – it's shorter, quicker, and way less annoying.

See also: *It's All in the Details*

30,000-Pound Gorilla

"What you do not know, is what you do not know it is, you do not know."

You Don't Know What You Don't Know

Wait, let's see if we've got this straight. You're saying that we don't know what we don't know… is that it?

Hmm, that's interesting… and very intuitive on your part. Thank you… we suppose.

Ugh, this phrase is annoying both on the surface and in the underlying uselessness. That is, this is one of those phrases that doesn't really need a replacement because it never needed to be uttered in the first place.

Yes, none of us knows whatever it is we do not know; just as none of us possess whatever it is we do not possess.

Quite Zen on some level.

No, strike that, this is really more of a Yoda saying. Something so simple and unnecessary that only Yoda could repeat it and make it sound important.

Certainly, Yoda would move the words around a bit and utter it like, "You do not know what it is you do not know."

Of course, since you're not Yoda, stop saying it in any order.

Replacement phrases: No replacement needed; just please stop saying it.

See also: *It Is What It Is*

Did We Miss One of Your Favorites?

Our goal from the beginning was to present the top 101 annoying things managers say; though, as you now know, we settled on 212.

Of course, even including this many irritating business sayings, we know we left more than a few off the list. If we missed one of your favorites (or least favorites), please send a note to Steve@AskTheManager.com – we're already busy compiling a new list for a follow-up book.

Steve's Other Books:

Sh*t Sandwich: Quick & Practical Success Lessons for Practically Anyone (2017)

Written in the same style as *30,000-Pound Gorilla* (albeit using saltier language), *Sh*t Sandwich* provides 83 short lessons crafted to entertain as it educates today's youth (and those who refuse to grow up) that life's really not all that fair… in fact, we should expect to eat our share of shit sandwiches along the way. That is, if we want to be successful.

Assumptive Selling: The Complete Guide to Selling More Vehicles for More Money to Today's Connected Customers (2018)

Assumptive Selling is nothing like *30,000-Pound Gorilla*! This one was written specifically for car dealers and their sales teams to help them successfully create better buying experiences for today's customers. Dealers who've adopted *Assumptive Selling* across their organizations enjoy improved sales and profits, lower employee turnover, and increased customer satisfaction.

Printed in Poland
by Amazon Fulfillment
Poland Sp. z o.o., Wrocław